THIS BOOK BELONGS TO:

_____

Because this tool is essential to creating a bigger future,

a reward is offered when returned to the owner. Please call:

_____

"What do you really want from life? What do you want to be? To all those seeking answers to these fundamental questions, Curtis Estes brings a profound but straightforward strategy in *Your Life by Design*. Peppered with personal examples, it's a practical guide for under- and overachievers alike—for anyone 'living by default.' This book is a lot like Curtis: motivational!"

— **JOHN E. SCHLIFSKE**, Chairman and CEO, Northwestern Mutual

"Your Life By Design presents a practical, workable, inspirational guide to planning your future rather than just reacting to it. From dreams to reality, put Curtis Estes' strategies to work for you!"

— **HARVEY MACKAY**, author of the #1 *New York Times* best-seller
Swim With The Sharks Without Being Eaten Alive

"To live the fullest life, it takes clear and continual sense of direction—not by chance but by design. This valuable book serves as a compelling wake-up call."

— **ROBERT K. COOPER,** author of the *New York Times* best-seller
Get Out of Your Own Way, The Other 90%, and *Executive E.Q.*

"Your Life by Design places significance where it belongs—on self awareness, aligned values, and an action plan. This book contains the key to transformation!"

— **MORRIS R. SHECHTMAN,** author of *Working Without a Net* and
Fifth Wave Leadership, speaker and chairman of Fifth Wave Leadership

"A rare and defining book that will awaken the voice inside of you that tells you to live a deeper, more powerful existence."

— **PHILIP TIRONE,** author of *7 Steps to a 720 Credit Score*

"*Your Life by Design* is a wake-up call to overachievers questioning the sacrifices they make in pursuit of greater success but at the expense of their personal happiness and wellbeing. Curtis is a master at helping people bring their vision and passion into balance and aligned with their lifestyle. I am blessed to have seen this first hand with extraordinarily successful people. The strategies are elegantly simple but have the ability to inspire radical change."

> — **JENNIFER KUSHELL**, co-author of the *New York Times* best-seller
> *Secrets of the Young & Successful* and co-founder of YSN.com
> (Your Success Network)

"Do yourself a favor and get two copies of *Your Life by Design*. Grab a pen and fill the first one with your plans for the future. Give the second one to the person you love most in the world."

> — **FRANK TIRELLI**, chairman and CEO of Deloitte Italy

"The Pyramid Flip and To Be List alone are worth much more than the cost of the book. I highly recommend you buy this book for yourself and your closest friends!"

> — **ROBERT PAGLIARINI**, financial motivator and author,
> *The Other 8 Hours* and *The Six-Day Financial Makeover:*
> *Transform Your Financial Life in Less Than a Week!*

"Whether you are dealing with a hardship, working to improve your own life, or looking to discover a better path to happiness, this is the book. Curtis has an inspiring outlook, jaw-dropping energy, and authentic love for everything he does, and his fresh perspective helps anyone lead a life by design and discover what it truly means to be happy."

> — **ANTHONY MARGULEAS**, president of Amalfi Estates

YOUR LIFE

A Step-by-Step Guide to Creating a Bigger Future

Curtis R. Estes

BIGGER FUTURES PRESS

an Intellectual Capital Corporation company

LOS ANGELES, CA

Fourth Edition 2015
Third Edition 2014
Second Edition 2010
First Edition 2008

Published by Bigger Futures Press,
an Intellectual Capital Corporation company
For orders, visit www.curtisestes.biz

978-0-9814786-1-6 | paperback
978-0-9814786-2-3 | ebook
Printed in the United States of America

Edited by Jocelyn Baker (www.ghostwritersanon.com)
Book design by Dotti Albertine (www.albertinebookdesign.com)
Cover design by Tony Laidig

To Kristi, Jordan, Vyvien, and Christian:
You are the reason behind my design.
You are my joy, strength, and dream come true.
Every effort, every pursuit, and every stride
are in honor of my commitments to you.

ACKNOWLEDGMENTS

OF THE MANY PEOPLE WHO HELPED DESIGN THIS BOOK, I want to acknowledge first and foremost my wife, Kristi, for providing love and logic throughout the writing and editing process; my mom for being what a mother should be, and more, for always supporting my dreams; my dad for always seeing opportunity in his midst and dreaming of a bright tomorrow; James Post for inspiring me to give of myself with joyful abandon; Bob Kerrigan for believing in me, especially when I did not; Dana Anderson for buying that margarita and modeling world-class generosity; Morrie Shechtman for telling me what I needed to hear, not what I wanted to hear; Dan Sullivan for being my Strategic Coach®; Conrad York, Michael Van Grinsven, and Lindsay Schmit for their tremendous support from Milwaukee; and Philip Tirone, Bryce Eddy, Robert Pagliarini and Ethan Frey for so bigheartedly taking time to review this manuscript. Thanks also to my Extraordinary Leaders Team for supporting my weekly breakthrough testing since February 1, 2009.

CONTENTS

CONTENTS

FOREWORD

WHEN I MET CURTIS, I didn't know about his talent, but I was immediately impressed by his energy and warmth. Since then, in addition to becoming one of my favorite entrepreneurs in Strategic Coach, he has become a great friend. And I know that my friendship with him will be increasingly positive for the rest of my life. What I have also discovered about Curtis is that he has marvelous strategic sense in designing and building his own life and career—and that he does the same for hundreds of other people who are his friends and clients.

Now, although it is not apparent from his happy, friendly manner, Curtis wants everyone to know that he has worked hard for everything he has achieved. But there's a big difference between just working hard and working smart. If you spend an hour with him, you immediately know that Curtis will out-plan and out-strategize everyone else in the marketplace. And, again, everything that he does for himself, he also does for others.

Which brings me to the subject of this book and the reason he wrote it.

Curtis Estes has hundreds of journals, binders, and files dedicated to drawing a connection between activities and outcomes. Want to know what he wore on December 21, 1990? Curtis can tell you: He wore a red button-down, a gray sweater, and blue jeans.

Why the copious notes? "I wanted to know whether my wardrobe affected my mood," he explained.

Curtis has journals that detail his favorite parts of each day, his life's highlights, his biggest dreams, his health, his income, and everything in between. By keeping these journals, Curtis can study the patterns in his life. From these patterns, he can then set goals to change behavior and realize different outcomes. (Of course, he keeps additional journals to track his goal-setting activities.)

In the years I have known him, Curtis has continually grown, progressed, and achieved in every part of his business and personal life. He has gone from being, in his words, "a run-of-the-mill financial planner" to being, in the judgment of many others, a truly unique lifetime strategic breakthrough partner. He's earning far more, working far less, having great fun at home and at work—and is a delight to everyone who meets him. Curtis's circle of friends is thousands of miles wide and expanding. The man is a ball of focused, kind, and caring energy that touches, shapes, and connects those who meet him.

All of these qualities come through in this book. *Your Life by Design* is a synthesis of the best tools Curtis has discovered during his journey. It lays out how Curtis always makes his future bigger, and by reading and using it, it will do the same for you.

— Dan Sullivan, founder and president, The Strategic Coach, Inc.

YOUR LIFE BY DESIGN

There is no passion to be found playing small, in settling for a life that is less than the one you are capable of living.
—Nelson Mandela

RECALL THAT FIRST MOMENT OF INSPIRATION when you graduated from college, landed that dream job, or first laid eyes upon your spouse. Your ambition was unlimited and your confidence unshakable. Perhaps you were thinking, *I will run this company. I will make millions. My life will overflow with success and happiness.*

Your future never seemed bigger than it did on that day. The energy was palpable. You could not fail.

And you didn't. Today, you are at the top of your game. You earn more than you ever imagined. You have an abundance of success. But despite all of this success, perhaps you do not have that same clarity of purpose. Something is missing; there's not that old spring in your step.

It is time to create a new picture of your future with fresh ambitions and an unshakable confidence that you can achieve the life you envision.

Let's rekindle the fire of earlier days when anything was possible. With the advantage of your experience, looking upward toward the stars, what would your ideal life look like?

Ideal Life Worksheet™

Grab a pen and take as much time as necessary to describe your ideal life. You might want to consider answers to such questions as: What does success look like? What characteristics do I see in others that I want to model?

Congratulations! Simply by writing down a few ideas for the future, you have created new neural pathways in your brain that will facilitate the fulfillment of your ideal life. These connections are the rails that you will fully form and deepen over the coming days by creating *Your Life by Design*™.

But before we get too far, let's make sure you know about the Overachiever Trap so that if you have fallen in, you can pull yourself out.

THE OVERACHIEVER TRAP

Difficulties elicit talents that in more fortunate circumstances would lie dormant.
　　　　　　—HORACE

ONLY THOSE WHO RISK GOING TOO FAR can possibly find out how far one can go." This is the creed of the overachiever. We push the limits, challenge ourselves, and set the bar high, holding ourselves to standards we never expect from the rest of the world. We constantly wish the day had more hours. We pass up sleep so we can be the early birds that catch the worm. We do not cut corners. Hard work, we remind ourselves, is the cornerstone of success, and we force ourselves to work longer, smarter, and faster.

The payoff for living this creed is high. Most of us have surpassed our financial expectations. Some of us are in the top one percent of wealthy Americans. We are entrepreneurs, executives, professionals, and philanthropists. We have made names for ourselves and enjoy recognition and admiration. On many levels, we represent the American dream. I, for one, grew up as a poor farm boy from a small agricultural town in Kansas where opportunities were not abundant. Today, I have built a successful entrepreneurial business[1] and consistently rank within the top one percent of my industry.

Those of us who have reached the highest echelons of career achievement are considered to be among the most successful in society. We are the superstars

---

1. For more information, visit **WWW.CURTISESTES.COM**.

whose biggest dreams are at our fingertips. We have reached a level of success that would allow us to retire early, pursue our dream careers, start charitable foundations, or whatever else we may choose. We are considered the lucky ones.

Yet many of us are teetering on tightropes of imbalance. Instead of pursuing our dreams and enjoying our hard-won success, we cling blindly to a routine whose aim we cannot recall. Far too common is the lawyer basking in the sunlight of her corner office, but deeply burdened by the discontent of an unfulfilling job that has somehow taken over her life; the businessman who longs for a family connection, yet for the past 10 years has failed to celebrate his wedding anniversaries; the city dweller running a furious race, exhausted from the hustle and bustle of the smoggy city, longing to breathe the salty ocean air while living in a quaint beach community.

Bradford D. Smart, Ph.D., author of *Topgrading* (Penguin Group Ltd., 2005), poignantly notes that most top managers and executives "lie awake at night, listening to their heartbeat: *thump-thump, thump-thump*. Worrying. Worrying about their performance, about company politics. About that … bar being raised." Not only do we lose sleep, we also miss our children's birthdays. Family trips turn into work as we lug our laptops and cell phones along for "vacations." We fail to attend weddings and family reunions. Our friends have long ago stopped counting on us for emotional support. After all, duty calls.

> **COACHING TIP:**
>
> *Determine whether you have fallen into the Overachiever Trap by visiting* WWW.CURTISESTES.BIZ *and taking the Life by Design Opportunities Finder*

This is the price many of us pay for living the creed of the overachiever. It is a mousetrap that seduces the overachiever with promises of wealth, success, fame, or glory. The pay*off* might be high, but so too is the pay*out*; indeed, it is too high a price. The cost does not justify the reward. It is a sacrifice instead of an even exchange, and it jeopardizes our ability to live lives that *feel* significant. Though the outside world might consider us the lucky ones, the truth is that we have traded fulfillment for professional success. We have sacrificed a balanced life for a more attractive balance sheet.

Why? While many of us have reached remarkable professional success, superstars are often guilty of losing sight of the answer to this simple, three-letter question: Why? Why are we working so hard?

Though we each have a different *why*, I can tell you one thing for certain: Money is not the answer. Most of us have long surpassed the need for financial security. So why do we place so much emphasis on the one area of life in which we are no longer needy?

This is a question I *can* answer. Most high-achievers are initially driven by a financial goal, but upon reaching this goal, they fail to define a new *why*. When I first moved to Los Angeles, I found myself rolling pennies so I could fill the gas tank to make it to my next appointment. I knew the answer to the question: *Why am I working so hard?* I worked long and hard hours because I needed money.

But I have moved past the urgency of this need. My life has grown to include a wife, three children, a successful business, and many friends. I enjoy a variety of hobbies and have access to ample opportunity. So shouldn't my *why* mature and progress in accordance with my life?

If you fail to reevaluate your *why* in tandem with the change in your circumstances, you will continue to be driven by the same siren call of our commercial society—a pursuit of money and material things. This reason likely *feels* artificial because it *is* artificial. You already have enough money, so you are desensitized to the joy you felt when you cashed your first big check. Even the newest BMW is not much more than a means of transportation six months after you drive it off the lot. If you do not update your *why* accordingly, replacing it with an authentic reason that drives your actions, you have no compelling motivation, and you are bound to be bored, frustrated, or dissatisfied.

So what now? If you have reached and surpassed your financial goals, you might believe that your past is bigger than your future, thinking you have accomplished it all simply because you have earned much money or created a successful and meaningful business. You might fail to remember a time when you wanted to accomplish so much that one lifetime did not seem enough, when you knew that life's possibilities are endless, that an I've-done-it-all attitude is rubbish.

How does this happen? How do the superstars with big dreams settle and compromise their expectations for their careers, their relationships, and their health, ending up with lives they did not design? The answer is as simple as this: By failing to design a life with as much intention, passion, and dedication as we pour into our careers, we will be destined to lives that are designed for us, created by external forces, people, or events. We will be destined to live by default. And the further away from our dreams that we move, the more desperate or hopeless we might feel.

Tragically, many of today's superstars are living by default. Caught in the day-to-day requirements of achieving professional success, these otherwise insightful individuals are often disconnected from other areas of their lives—the spouses, children, friends, and hobbies for which they never make time. These take a backburner to "more pressing issues," like staying on top of email. And while the outside world is lauding them for their professional success, these individuals are wondering why they feel disconnected and unfulfilled. *Isn't there supposed to be more to life? Why do I still feel a sense of hollow dissatisfaction? Is something missing?*

To be sure, something *is* missing. A successful life includes a successful career, but it is *more* than a successful career. To fill your life with passion, you must dig deep and discover what you are passionate about—and then design your life to achieve that purpose. No client account, no phone call, no professional emergency can take precedence over this. To fail is to sentence yourself to live a life by default, to never discover or realize those goals that would afford you fulfillment and a sense of completeness.

Your Life by Design™ helps overachievers identify their values and then align their lives with these values through a specific goal-setting process. The result is a personal transformation that helps superstars design—and achieve—a life as successful and meaningful as their careers.

When I was 10 years old, my life careened out of control when my family home burned to the ground on Christmas Day. Without fire insurance, my family was left with nothing. We moved into a trailer and were given clothes from our church, the Salvation Army, and friends. This was one of several grim times in my life. Over the next few years, my family suffered through the dregs of financial instability. To help keep my family afloat, I worked alongside my mother and sister at the local McDonald's. My life felt deeply precarious; at times, it seemed hopeless.

And yet I was fortunate to have a strong internal compass, even during this difficult time. An avid daydreamer, I began designing my escape plan by setting goals and visualizing attainment of these goals. While working at the McDonald's grill, I thought about the movie *The Secret of My Succe$s* in which a young Michael J. Fox plays a hardworking man from rural Kansas who dreams of climbing the ranks of a multi-million dollar company in New York City. He was well educated, savvy, and courageous, but because of his limited experience, no one would hire him. Still, he landed a job in the mailroom and quickly carved his own original, authentic path, eventually soaring to success.

I was already a believer in hard work, and this character further affirmed my belief that **strategy holds unseen power**. I realized that when preparation meets opportunity, a person can create his own luck. Goals were the escape route that would take me from a place of apathy and happenstance to a solid place of intentionality and hope. Identifying my values, and then conceptualizing those goals that would allow me to achieve these values, made everything else in my life seem not only manageable, but also temporary.

As humbling as it was standing at the McDonald's grill flipping burgers next to my mother and younger sister, the experience served as a launching pad by forcing me to dream about a better future. Tom and Marilyn Dobski, the franchise's owners, modeled the values of hard work and kindness. They led by example, trusted the employees to become their best, and encouraged me to dream big. Not long after I learned to drive, Tom entrusted me with his beautiful new car to make a delivery to another McDonald's franchise. I was King of the Road that afternoon, feeling what it was like to travel in style. Later, the Dobskis awarded me a generous scholarship after learning that I received a summer internship in Washington D.C.

Tom and Marilyn Dobski inspired me to thoughtfully and intentionally imagine moving beyond my circumstances. Since then, I have been in a constant state of evolution, pushing, exploring, moving, and reaching far beyond any circumstantial or emotional limitations. This internal discovery process is what I hope to share with you. Through a series of simple, fast, and efficient steps, *Your Life by Design™* will guide you through the process of finding your vision and then turning it into a reality.

1. First, you will develop clarity about your dreams, building a bigger **vision** for your future through a personalized, value-based process that will set the foundation from which all else will rise.

2. Once your vision is established, you will create a specific, actionable **strategy** that allows the vision to come to fruition.

3. Then, you will **implement** your strategic plan with ease throughout the inner workings of your life, ensuring that your environment has abundant and fertile soil to support and enhance your vision.

4. Finally, you will see **transformational results** using your *Life By Design Manual*™ to ensure success and enjoy the journey of living *Your Life by Design*™.

To give yourself a taste of what is to come by designing your life, ask yourself these questions: Wouldn't it be amazing if I could make a great contribution to the world? If I could spend more time with my loved ones? If I could pursue that passion, travel to that country, or live that dream? What would my ideal life look like? Let's build upon your thoughts from the Ideal Life Worksheet™ on page 2. **In the pages ahead, you will make a discovery called *Your Life by Design*™, and it is the secret to *your* success.**

Throughout this book, you will find helpful, progressive activities culminating in creation of your *Life by Design Manual*.™ You will see how your cumulative efforts create an elegant solution for obtaining clarity and seeing amazing results. Your *Life by Design Manual*™ is an evolving and dynamic blueprint that serves as inspiration and a constant reminder that you control the design of your life.

Now, let's get started by exploring and building your vision.

THE SIX VISION-BUILDING ACTIVITIES

BIGGER VISION

SPECIFIC STRATEGY DRIVEN BY THE COMPELLING WHY

EXACTING IMPLEMENTATION

TRANSFORMING RESULTS

THE SIX VISION-BUILDING ACTIVITIES

Dream lofty dreams, and as you dream, so you shall become. Your vision is the promise of what you shall one day be, your ideal is the prophecy of what you shall at last unveil.
—James Allen

TAKE A MOMENT TO LOOK BACK AT THE DESCRIPTION of your ideal life from Ideal Life Worksheet™ on page 2. Perhaps it looks something like this: Your career represents all that you want and nothing that you do not want. After 20 years of marriage, you and your spouse still act like honeymooners. Your relationship with your children, siblings, and parents is strong. You have plenty of time to travel, pursue hobbies, and spend time with close friends. Each day is more fulfilling than the last and better than you could have imagined.

Now consider the contrast between your ideal life and reality. Like an electrical shock, which occurs when two radically opposed polarities come into contact with one another, your discontent worsens as the magnitude of the opposing forces intensifies. The greater the difference between your ideal life and reality, the more alarming your circumstances become, and the greater the shock. This is the bleak and stark reality of living by default. At best, it is dissatisfying, boring, or incomplete. At worst, it can be startling, debilitating, and dismal. Think, for instance, of the people you know who are financially successful but chained to jobs, missing dinner with family members, and glued to their computers and smartphones while on vacation.

The fundamental difference between living by default and living by design is that to live by design is to live *purposefully*. It is to define a vision for what you want from life and then to systematically identify and pursue the goals necessary to make that vision a reality.

But how do we determine what we want from life? What we really, passionately want to get from our days on Earth? The answer is not obvious. Indeed, it is not even clear how to go about figuring out the answer.

We have all had the experience of wanting something—a new gadget, a luxury vehicle—only to discover upon obtaining it that it really was not what we had hoped it would be. The reality does not always match the dream. If we are to lead a rich and fulfilling life, we cannot allow this to happen with our vision. When we decide on a vision for our life, we must know that its achievement will bring us fulfillment.

But how do we first figure out where we want to be so that we can later determine how to get there?

In this section of *Your Life by Design*™, you learn how to design your life and prioritize your time by crafting a vision that drives all your activities. Creating a bigger vision for your future is the first and foremost step in creating *Your Life by Design*™.

A proper vision enables us to take proactive steps to achieve it. A life lived by default is a life lived in reaction. It is a life spent doing what you *should* do or *have* to do rather than what you *want* to do. Living by design, remember, is living purposefully, taking intentional steps that drive you closer to your goal. To design your life is to spend less time doing what you *should* do (often defined by valueless societal norms) and more time doing what you *want* to do (those things that inspire you as they are the springboard to your dreams).

During college, I created a calendar system called Time CREations™. This was my first entrepreneurial endeavor. The purpose of the Time CREations™ calendar was to monitor and track not only my day-to-day activities but also the emotion and energy attached to each of these activities. I tracked what I did, the new people I met, and even the clothing I wore. I then attributed a numerical score that indicated my positive and negative emotions that were attached to each activity.

Curtis Estes's Time CREations™ calendar from Thursday, December 21, 1990

Emotional/ Feeling Scale	Timetable	Event	
	8:00		**Day's Priorities**
	8:30		Schedule appointment with Tom
	9:00		Change oil in car
	9:30		Review psychology notes
	10:00		Write letter to Jen and Ken
6	10:30	Planning meeting/M. Cummings	
8	11:00	Meeting with Tom to discuss discipline	
	11:30		
	12:00		**Call**
4	12:30	Help move Ed out of dorm	Tom
	1:00		Mike
10	1:30	Cruise KC with Jennifer	Social Security office
	2:00		
10	2:30	Yani exhibit at Nelson art gallery	
	3:00		**Day's Fashion**
	3:30		Gray sweater
10	4:00	Cappuccino with friends	Red button down
7	4:30	Shop at Seville Square	Blue jeans
	5:00		
	5:30		
3	6:00	Car appointment	**Day's Goals**
	6:30		Get to know Sally well
	7:00	Dinner with Sally	
	7:30		**Expenditures**
	8:00		$2 at Nelson Art Gallery
	8:30		$10 for lunch and cappuccino
	9:00		$150 oil change and unexpected
10	9:30		maintenance
	10:00		$35 at Dos Hombres
	10:30		
	11:00		
	12:00		

The goal of Time CREations™ was to explore the moments, people, and circumstances that made me feel best. More than creating a reminder of the pink Ralph Lauren jacket I proudly sported during the '80s, the calendar allowed me to recognize the situations I embraced with joy, and those that caused anxiety, fear, or other negative emotions. The calendar's name, Time CREations™, was not only a play on my initials, but also served as a reminder that it was up to me to create the ways in which I spent my time. It was up to me to design my life.

While my Time CREations™ invention did not reward me with millions (or even hundreds) of dollars, the essence of this exercise taught me something priceless: the intrinsic value of time—not just the importance of the hours ticking away, but also that the way I spend my time solely dictates the fulfillment I experience in my life. We have access to no greater or more limited resource than time, yet many well intended, highly successful, and disciplined individuals continue to waste time away. I do not imagine that many of my readers are sitting idly on the couch while munching potato chips and watching reruns of their favorite sitcom (at least not regularly). But how many of us spend time at bureaucratic meetings or random events that we feel we ought to be a part of when, in fact, we would rather be spending time with our families or somewhere else where we could be leveraging our talent to create value?

Take a moment to gauge your level of energy right now. Are you a ten or a one? On fire or hibernating? And what about your level of focus? Are you in the zone or zoned out? Do you take time to check in to see whether you are in the game, or do you simply wander through life haphazardly?[1]

At every interaction and in every moment, you get to choose how much you want to get out of life. By designing your life and paying close attention to the details of your life, you can choose to be 100 percent alive.

Far too many of us have become accidental tourists in our own lives, allowing happenstance to be our guide and carrying the heavy baggage of imposed action and fear. Most of us have days that are filled with activities we *should* do. Living

---

1. According to Robert Cooper, if you take the time to "check in" and self-rate your energy level and focus level, you will automatically increase both simply because you will be placing attention on these two important components of living a life by design.

dangerously out of balance, many superstars are bound by the self-imposed chains of the *shoulds* instead of the *wants*. These chains blend into the backdrop of our lives until many of us no longer realize that we have control over our *shoulds*, and we unknowingly become keepers of our own discontent, serving and crafting our own sentence by the *shoulds* that exist within our schedules. We simply forget that we can control the way we spend our time.

Later, we will talk in detail about the importance of schedules. We will see that a person's schedule represents his life, and it is therefore the single most important tool in creating *Your Life by Design™*. Let me reinforce this statement: As simple as it sounds, a person's schedule is an exact measure of how he spends his time, whether he will love or hate his days, whether his life is filled with *wants* or with *shoulds*. The small, day-to-day moments of a schedule are the footprints of life. With precision and clarity, they determine your detours and ascensions, resolving whether you are on a path to greatness. Simply by reflecting on my Time CREations™ calendar from college, I can remember what my life looked like, how happy I was, how often I was content with my life, and how often I was doing what I *should* be doing instead of what I *wanted* to be doing.

On the following page, take a moment to reflect on your schedule.

Wants Versus *Shoulds*

Find a 24-hour block of time that reflects your typical day. Take an honest account of the details within this day. Classify each activity into one of two categories: those you believe you want to be doing that express and leverage your highest ideals, most important priorities, and move you toward your ideal life; and those you believe you should be doing but perhaps are not essential or could be delegated. You can think of your wants versus your shoulds as those activities you dislike doing versus those activities you love doing.

Now, list the wants that fill your schedule, as well as the shoulds.

Wants **in my schedule**	*Shoulds* **in my schedule**
(activities I love)	(activities I dislike)
_____	_____
_____	_____
_____	_____
_____	_____
_____	_____
_____	_____
_____	_____
_____	_____
_____	_____
_____	_____
_____	_____
_____	_____
_____	_____

Now consider where you were 10, 20, 30, or 40 years ago and how you spent the majority of your time. Perhaps consider your college days, or the earliest days of your career. Since that time, you have reached greater success. You have more resources. You have more money. You know more people. You have bigger opportunities. Couldn't you be doing what you want to do now, more than ever before? This is your time to pursue your opportunities and dreams. If you found fulfillment before you had loving, supportive families, blessed careers, and a budding pocketbook, certainly you can find it now!

By inventing the Time CREations™ system and subsequently identifying my own *wants* and *shoulds*, I began living intentionally. I began seeking situations that resulted in positive emotions and trying to remove those that caused negative emotions. This became my first step toward understanding the influence I had over my life. Since then, many steps have followed—steps that have taken me far from rural Kansas, far from default, and straight into the heart of a life of my choosing, a life of my design. But creating this fulfillment has required a deep understanding of myself established through disciplined introspection. Specifically, it has required a discovery of my vision. Without a clear idea as to where I am going (my vision), I do not have a clear direction as to which opportunities to pursue, and which strategies will most quickly bring me closer to my goals.

For most business owners and superstars, creating a vision is not a novel concept, and you have likely crafted your share. But I want to warn you against one problem that keeps many from being effective: imbalance. Imbalance is among the most common saboteurs inherent in well-intended visions. For a vision to be successful, it must integrate all primary areas of life. When our visions are deep and integrated, we are able to remain committed to activities that support these visions. Likewise, we are able to walk away from those activities that do not support this future.

Take, for example, David, a businessman who places significant value on his family. In fact, his family is his top priority: His values include playing a major role in the development of his children, attending his children's sporting events, and keeping the romance alive with his wife. At the same time, David wants continued growth in his business. When a business opportunity arises that requires constant travel but will surely afford this man substantial professional growth, how does he evaluate his choices? Unless he has an integrated vision in place, one that simultaneously supports both values (building his business and being a family man), he will face inner turmoil and will likely believe that he must sacrifice one of his dreams in exchange for another.

But with an integrated vision, the choice becomes obvious, if not easy. "When our romantic commitments are deep," writes Robert K. Cooper, Ph.D., in *Get*

Out of Your Own Way (Crown Business, 2006), "we say *no* to other involvements that might compromise these commitments. When we are financially committed to some goal—buying a home, let's say—we say *no* to expenditures that stand in the way of attaining that goal."

When David considers his vision, he recognizes that the business opportunity would compromise his relationship with his wife and children. The choice, therefore, is obvious: Pass on this particular opportunity and pursue other means of building his career. Though sacrificing his family might reward David with greater career satisfaction, his other values would be unmet, and he would feel unfulfilled. As well, he would close the door to other opportunities that might support both values.

Though some might be fortunate to have an epiphany at 3 a.m. or while taking a shower, most (including me) must mine for their visions as aggressively as they built their business. Vast resources counsel us to create a vision. As a life-long student of transformational work, I have completed most of these exercises. Some have been helpful, others not. In respecting my readers, who are already limited in time, I have refined these tools, creating gems that are suited to the superstar and fashioned to provide the fastest and most efficient outcome.

In the pages that follow, you will find a range of activities that will help you uncover your vision:

- Vision-Building Activity #1—Kindle Your Energy by Making Your Highlight Reel™

- Vision-Building Activity #2—The Pyramid Flip™

- Vision-Building Activity #3—Identifying Your Unique Ability®

- Vision Building Activity #4—The To Be List™

- Vision-Building Activity #5—Your Personal Legacy™

- Vision-Building Activity #6—Creating the Bigger Vision™

These activities will provide you with the tools, methods, and techniques to excavate your most sacred and aligned values, later enabling you to intentionally shape the moments and details of your life. Ultimately, the vision you create will be one that is representative of whom you want to be. Truly understanding and aligning your values and your vision allows you to become more effective in your life. As you embark on this journey, empowerment, ownership, and deep, abiding joy will meet you in unexpected hours.

VISION-BUILDING ACTIVITY #1

—Kindle Your Energy by Making Your Highlight Reel™

> *At the peak of tremendous and victorious effort, while the blood is pounding in your head, all suddenly becomes quiet within you. Everything seems clearer and whiter than ever before, as if great spotlights had been turned on. At that moment, you have the conviction that you contain all the power in the world, that you are capable of everything, that you have wings. There is no more precious moment in life than this, the white moment.*
>
> —Yuri Vlasov, Soviet Weightlifter

THE EASIEST, MOST OBVIOUS PLACE TO FIND OUR VISION is by looking at the biggest and boldest moments of our lives, the memories that carry spiritual and emotional sustenance. This exercise consists of asking yourself: *When have I felt most alive? During which moments of my life have I felt optimum energy and peak performance?*

Too many superstars measure their lives based on their last 24-hour experience, taking limited, tight, and compartmentalized accounts of their successes or failures, living only with the emotions and successes of the past day. This activity, on the other hand, requires you to record the history of your shining, profound, soul-awakening, and joy-filled moments, regardless of how big or small these moments might be. By considering the best moments of your life, you take note of what you were doing and, from this, you can glean why these events recorded in your memory are significant. This information, synthesized as your Highlight Reel™, will feed into your process of creating a vision.

When I created my Highlight Reel™, I noticed a trend in the types of activities that occurred. Namely, I noted such events as running for student government in college as significant, even though my life has taken me far from these years. But I felt alive and "in the zone" during this experience. When I asked myself what it was about this event, I realized that I loved meeting new people and connecting with them, learning about how their objectives could be met by my platform. I have carried this same passion with me throughout my life, and it appears as a trend on my Highlight Reel™. For instance, one of my highlights is, "Envisioning teaching 500 students weekly in Bible Study Fellowship." Though this might seem quite different than campaigning for student government, it shares some common denominators: connecting with people, sharing ideas, and serving as a leader.

The purpose of the Highlight Reel™ is to assist you in the creation of your vision by helping you reflect on those proud, happy moments that you most treasure. In this way, the Highlight Reel™ inspires you to create more of these moments, and like the Pyramid Flip™ (Activity #2) and Your Personal Legacy™ (Activity #5), it clarifies who you want to be, while reminding you of those times you felt the most proud and fulfilled.

To complete the Highlight Reel Worksheet™, take an honest and thoughtful account of the most memorable, significant, and transforming moments (people, places, and circumstances) of your life. Write down these moments as they occur to you, without concern for chronological order. A partial list of my Highlight Reel™ is included as an example.

You will notice that my Highlight Reel™ comprises obvious milestones, such as my wedding and the birth of my children, as well as seemingly trivial events. Being the first on the dance floor might not seem significant to an outside observer. The Highlight Reel™ is deeply personal. As I mentioned, it is intended to extract the most poignant moments and prompt thought into the types of activities that you enjoy. A seemingly trivial event might hold large significance because it holds some greater meaning to you.

Curtis Estes's Highlight Reel™ (a partial list)

- Recommitting my life to Christ at Big Bear Koinonia retreat with Steve Marsh.
- Proposing to Kristi on my knee at San Ysidro Ranch under a star-filled sky.
- Proclaiming "I will" to Kristi in our wedding ceremony.
- The glorious births of Jordan, Vyvien, and Christian!
- Participating in Presidential Classroom in high school during my first trip to Washington D.C.
- Earning the Heritage Foundation Summer internship.
- Profiting through scholarships to college.
- Campaigning for University of Kansas Student Senate at campus bus stops.
- Being the first on the dance floor for "Sunshine and Rain."
- Starting Honors Floor as a Resident Assistant leading freshman.
- Leading Esprit de Corps at 9:58 a.m. for "Students Serious About Success."
- Conquering Series 7 and CFP by studying and acing the exams.
- Founding the Sunset Club to connect young professionals while having a great time.
- Stepping into the crystal-clear ocean at my first Club Med in Turks and Caicos.
- Being exposed to great restaurants with ridiculous wine lists while dining with Bob and Keith.
- Honing my goals and action plan for the first time with Peter Greider.
- Delivering Fastrack and Agency speeches, getting the standing ovation from the audience of 6,000 in Chicago.
- Power skiing with Todd Tauzin.
- Life building with E. Dan Smith and Philip X. Tirone.
- Reading inspiring books such as *The Bible, The Count of Monte Cristo*, and *Les Misérables*.
- Collecting beautiful art from each vacation.
- Running through Paris.
- Swimming one mile without drowning.
- Being among the youngest Bel Air Country Club members and Whitworth University trustees.

- Envisioning teaching 500 students weekly in Bible Study Fellowship.
- Learning about myself with the help of Morrie, Barbara, Margi, Sherie, Robert, Parker, and the Kolbe test.
- Receiving the gold key to the Secret Table at the Cheese Store of Beverly Hills.
- Writing letters to my infant children while on business trips.
- Co-chairing the Bel Air Presbyterian Church "Changing Lives for Christ" Campaign in raising $25 million.
- Published second edition of *Your Life by Design*.
- Founded the LA Suitcase Party raising money for amazing charities like the Children's Hospital, Cloud and Fire, HOLA, the educational foundation of the Grammy Museum and the Youth Business Alliance, all by sending friends on private jets.
- Launch 12 Leaders with Robert Cooper on 12/12/12.
- Thanks to Dave Fenton, began Miracle Mornings with Silence, Affirmations, Visualization, Exercise, Reading, and Journaling.
- Completed first five years of Extraordinary Leaders Team weekly breakthrough testing.
- Beginning second trimester of my Life by Design at 45 toward age 132 in the year 2100.
- First half Iron Man six months after first sprint triathlon when I hadn't previously thought I could do the swim; monthly first Friday at 5 a.m. triathlons since.
- Amazing Lifebook weekend with Kristi and more intentional focus on becoming the best version of ourselves than ever before.
- Following Jeff Reeter's example, I love marking up my second One Year Bible with the goal of working through an additional Bible every year so that I can give one to all my kids and grand kids creating a testimonial legacy.
- Begin standing weekly 6 a.m. Inner Circle Calls with Ethan and Phil.
- Spending Tuesday and Thursday mornings in the Classroom of Silence – splashing through the surf at sunrise.
- Joining the California Club after first being rejected and 12 years later resigning because my goals for frugality exceeded my pride in membership.

- Living my goal for being rich toward God by increasing our tithe by 1% each year.
- Invited to help Peter Diamandis create a transformational community for his Abundance 360 conference as the first founding advisory board member.
- Published fourth edition of *Your Life by Design*.

Though the purpose of your Highlight Reel™ is to help you identify those activities that stand out as significant, thereby moving you one step closer to identifying your vision, it is important to note that the Highlight Reel™ also serves as an important reminder of who you are and how far you have come. This information will be vital as we move through the process, so keep your Highlight Reel™ close at hand.

Create your own Highlight Reel™ on the following page.

Highlight Reel Worksheet™

VISION-BUILDING ACTIVITY #2

—The Pyramid Flip™

Deep within man dwell those slumbering powers; powers that would astonish him, that he never dreamed of possessing; forces that would revolutionize his life if aroused and put into action.
—ORISON SWETT MARDEN

LIKE THE TIME CREATIONS™ CALENDAR, the purpose of the Pyramid Flip™ is to help you hone in on what captures your best quality of life by identifying those activities and moments that are working the best, as well as those that are not working at all. We all have activities we love doing, those that give us energy and inspire us to further greatness. Yet, most highly successful people spend only 5 to 15 percent of their time doing such activities. Instead, most of us find our calendars filled with activities that we do not want to do. Sure, we might excel in these activities, but we are not passionate about them. This misallocation of our time creates what Dan Sullivan of the Strategic Coach® calls a "Ceiling of Complexity" which sabotages our forward progression and breeds insidious discouragement.

A secret to success is setting up your calendar and environment so that you are able to spend at least 50 percent of your time in the activities that you love and excel at doing. Aligning your life in this way will produce "genius level" results over time with unparalleled satisfaction and ease. Eventually, *Your Life by Design*™ directs you through the process of making this transition, replacing dissatisfying activities with ones that bring pleasure, satisfaction, joy, and growth.

For now, the Pyramid Flip™ asks you to start by filling out the Pyramid Worksheet: The Present™ to identify those activities that currently fill your schedule, identifying those that provide a high quality of life as "penthouse" activities and those that detract from a strong quality of life as either "safe house" or "outhouse" activities. This tool will help you further distinguish the *shoulds* from the *wants*.

Curtis Estes's Pyramid Worksheet: The Present™

HELPING
SUPERSTARS
ENVISION BIGGER FUTURES
• BE MY CLIENTS' STRATEGIC
BREAKTHROUGH PARTNER • RUNNING
FIRE TRAILS, 10KS, MOUNTAIN BIKING
AND TRIATHLONS • MEETING NEW PEOPLE
• CONNECTING LIKE-MINDED PEOPLE • HELPING
PEOPLE SET AND ACCOMPLISH GOALS
• WORKING WITH ENTHUSIASTIC, MOTIVATED PEOPLE
• CAMPAIGNING AND POLITICS • PUBLIC SPEAKING TO BIG AUDIENCES
• SWIMMING AND BIKING WITH THE KIDS
• MEMORIZING PHILIPPIANS FROM THE BIBLE

PENTHOUSE | Activities I Love

• EXERCISING ON THE ELLIPTICAL MACHINE
• PREPARING THE PERSONAL NEEDS ANALYSIS
• PHONING
• WEIGHT-LIFTING
• PACKING FOR TRIPS

SAFEHOUSE | Activities I Neither Dislike or Love

• DETAIL WORK LIKE FILING
• LAUNDRY
• SWEEPING THE KITCHEN FLOOR
• READING THE TAX CODE
• HOME FIX-IT PROJECTS
• EXERCISING ON THE STAIRMASTER
• HIRING AND MANAGEMENT

OUTHOUSE | Activities I Dislike

At the bottom of the pyramid is the **outhouse**, which is dark, dank, and uninspiring, filled with *shoulds*. The base level of the pyramid represents the activities of life that you do not enjoy and likely do not do well. These tasks typically drain, fade, and sabotage your efforts, promoting a lesser self. Later, when creating a plan to achieve the vision (Section 2), these activities will be the first to eliminate as we develop strategies that will help you delegate these tasks and/ or cut them out of your life entirely. But first, you must establish what tasks, responsibilities, and actions imprison your energy level at its lowest and weakest form. To do so, here are some questions to ponder:

1. *What tasks do I wish I never had to do again?*

2. *What tasks cause me to habitually procrastinate?*

3. *What tasks cause me the most anxiety or frustration?*

4. *During what tasks do I have a bad attitude?*

Turn to page 35 to fill in your outhouse activities in the provided Pyramid Worksheet: The Present™.

In the middle of the pyramid is the **safe house**, which represents those activities that you are able to accomplish, often with ease and excellence, but not necessarily with enthusiasm. These tasks do not typically hinder your efforts and will not harm you. Yet they must be monitored and controlled. Activities in the safe house are often the easiest to mismanage because they do not normally cause direct suffering. Since we may feel moderately content operating at this level, the safe house can lead to complacency. Whereas the drudgery of the outhouse incites immediate action, the safe house feels comfortable and acceptable. Beware of this safety! As we know from our professional achievements, successful living requires us to push beyond our comfort zone, to take risks, to grow. Only then can we move from passive comfort to passionate achievement. To identify the activities in which you feel safe but uninspired and unchallenged, ask yourself the following questions:

1. *During what activities do I feel like I am going through the motion?*

2. *What activities are easy but not adding value to my life?*

3. *What activities do I consistently rank as low priority?*

4. *What activities feel safe but uninspired?*

Turn to page 35 to fill in your safe house activities in the Pyramid Worksheet: The Present™.

On some levels, I would rather be operating in the outhouse than in the safe house. When in the outhouse, I am aware that I want to move toward the light, that I want out of the outhouse, and that I must find a way to transition out of negative, draining, and depressing activities and into those that are inspiring. In the outhouse, we often daydream and imagine what the penthouse feels or looks like. But in the safe house, many dreams are put on hold, and we simply go through the motions, feeling neither pain nor exuberance. It is here, in the safe house, that we must be particularly aware and vigilant, for we are far more likely to get stuck in the safe house than we are in the outhouse.

To be sure, we do have to spend time participating in safe house activities. I neither love nor hate exercising. But this is an activity that I cannot delegate and that I must do to enjoy a great quality of life. Still, I consider ways to leverage this time. For example, I set up a television, DVR, and DVD player in front of my elliptical machine so that I can be entertained while I am exercising. The danger of the safe house is when *all* of our time is spent there. We can forget what living in the penthouse feels like, instead thinking that the safe house is as good as it gets. (Remember this saying: The *good* is often the enemy of the *great*.)

Our ultimate goal is the **penthouse**. The peak of the pyramid represents the space where light and energy abound. The penthouse holds those activities that you love doing—that challenge you, motivate you, and help you grow. Most likely, you are especially skilled in these areas, and your excellence contributes to your success.

The goal of the Pyramid Flip™, as the name suggests, is to flip your pyramid so that most of your time is spent in the penthouse rather than the outhouse and safe house. Ideally, you should spend as much time as possible in the penthouse. In subsequent chapters, we discuss activities that will help you make the transition from the outhouse to the penthouse. For now, we want to define those activities, tasks, and moments that move you closer to the penthouse. To identify penthouse activities, ask yourself the following questions:

1. *If I had nothing scheduled for the rest of today, what would I love to do?*

2. *During what tasks do I feel most alive?*

3. *If failure were not an option, what would I do?*

4. *What activities cause me to feel the most inspired and energized?*

Turn to page 35 to fill in your penthouse activities in the provided Pyramid Worksheet: The Present™.

For now, your pyramid looks like a traditional pyramid, with most of the room at the bottom two-thirds of the pyramid. A lot of your time is likely spent in the outhouse or the safe house, while only a small percentage is likely spent in the penthouse.

Pyramid Worksheet: The Present™

PENTHOUSE | Activities I Love

SAFEHOUSE | Activities I Neither Dislike or Love

OUTHOUSE | Activities I Dislike

Ideally we want to flip the pyramid to allow greater space in the penthouse than in the outhouse. The goal of identifying our personal pyramid is to allow our penthouse to be our common, everyday living space. We want to spend as much time as possible in this sun-drenched area and avoid the outhouse at all costs. You do not want a small penthouse, but a big one; you do not want to spend a little time in the penthouse, you want to spend almost *all* your time in the penthouse. Remember: life should be *lived* in the penthouse.

Curtis Estes's Flipped Pyramid Worksheet: The Ideal™

PENTHOUSE | Activities I Love

- HELPING SUPERSTARS ENVISION BIGGER FUTURES
- BE MY CLIENTS' STRATEGIC BREAKTHROUGH PARTNER
- RUNNING FIRE TRAILS, 10KS, MOUNTAIN BIKING AND TRIATHLONS
- MEETING NEW PEOPLE • CONNECTING LIKE-MINDED PEOPLE
- CAMPAIGNING/POLITICS • HELPING PEOPLE SET/ACCOMPLISH GOALS
- WORKING WITH ENTHUSIASTIC, MOTIVATED PEOPLE
- PUBLIC SPEAKING TO BIG AUDIENCES
- SWIMMING AND BIKING WITH THE KIDS
- MEMORIZING PHILIPPIANS FROM THE BIBLE

SAFEHOUSE | Activities I Neither Dislike or Love

- DELEGATED THE PERSONAL NEEDS ANALYSIS TO STAFF
- HIRED FANTASTIC MARKETING ASSISTANT FOR PHONING
- PARTNERED WITH SEAN TO ENJOY WEIGHTLIFTING
- CONNECTED TV AND DVD TO ELLIPTICAL
- CREATED STANDARD PACKING LIST

OUTHOUSE | Activities I Dislike

- HIRED HOUSEKEEPER FOR DETAIL WORK
- RECEIVED TAX CODE UPDATES FROM ADVANCED PLANNING DEPT.
- HIRED HANDYMAN
- GAVE STAIRMASTER TO CHARITY
- RELY ON OFFICE MANAGER FOR HIRING AND MANAGEMENT

Now, flip your own pyramid, writing in outhouse activities at the bottom of the upside-down pyramid provided (Flipped Pyramid Worksheet: The Ideal™), and filling in the spacious penthouse with activities you love doing. The point of flipping this pyramid is twofold: First, like all activities in this section, you are working to identify your vision, which will comprise primarily penthouse activities. Second, you want to identify those outhouse and safe house activities that you can stop doing, delegate, or otherwise strategize to eliminate, which we will do in Vision-Building Activity #6—Creating the Bigger Vision™. (Realize that continuing to do what makes you crazy essentially imprisons your future. Your challenge is to free your future from the tyranny of the past.) For now, simply flip your pyramid as a symbolic gesture, thinking of the way you can transition into a life where most of your time is spent in the penthouse. Later, in the next section, we will make plans to delegate or eliminate many of the activities in your outhouse and safe house.

The flipped pyramid is the ideal, and in subsequent pages, we will work to transition your day-to-day activities so that your daily schedule reflects this inverted pyramid. In the next chapter you will get even more clarity on how to spend time in the penthouse by identifying your Unique Ability®.

Flipped Pyramid Worksheet: The Ideal™

PENTHOUSE | Activities I Love

SAFEHOUSE | Activities I Neither Dislike or Love

OUTHOUSE | Activities I Dislike

VISION-BUILDING ACTIVITY #3

—Identifying Your Unique Ability®[1]

> *When you engage in a work that taps your talent and fuels your*
> *passion—that rises out of a great need in the world that you feel*
> *drawn by conscience to meet—therein lies your voice, your calling,*
> *your soul's code.*
> —STEPHEN COVEY

DAN SULLIVAN, FOUNDER OF STRATEGIC COACH®, spends much time with his clients discussing their Unique Ability®, a phrase he coined to describe that unique combination of talent and passion that reflects not only what a person loves to do, but also what he is good at doing. Since Sullivan has introduced the concept, it has spread like wildfire, launching countless entrepreneurs to higher levels of achievement. This section provides a brief explanation of the Unique Ability®, but to truly understand and capitalize on your own Unique Ability®, sign up for Strategic Coach®(WWW.STRATEGICCOACH.COM) or read *Unique Ability®* by Catherine Nomura, Julia Waller, and Shannon Waller.

The purpose of the Unique Ability® is to reach an understanding of that specific component of your being that allows you to achieve and, at the same time, reach fulfillment, thereby providing you with a balanced life. To understand your Unique Ability®, you will need to broaden your perspective and seek

---

1. Unique Ability® is a registered trademark and copyrighted work owned by
The Strategic Coach, Inc. All rights reserved. Used with written permission.

insight from your friends, family, and co-workers to discover what it is that they believe drives you. When you see yourself in a mirror or a photograph, much of the depth, color, and layers go unseen. You see only one side of the picture. The same principle applies when evaluating your strengths, weaknesses, and contribution to the world. Another person's experience of you will undoubtedly be subtly different than your own, and will help you gain a fuller picture of your abilities. Ask your friends, family members, and colleagues questions such as:

1. *What am I best at?*

2. *What do you think I am exceptionally skilled at doing, considering my attitude, energy and enthusiasm?*

3. *What are my strengths and when do I shine?*

4. *What is the single attribute that most accurately describes me?*

Gaining this insight allows you to see sides of you that are present in every relationship, which leads to a greater understanding of what drives you. By working with Dan Sullivan and reading *Unique Ability®*, I was able to narrow my Unique Ability® to the following: My Unique Ability® is meeting, befriending, and connecting people to help them create bigger futures, reaching their most amazing future sooner than anyone expects.

Honing in on my Unique Ability® reminded me of those things I do not like doing or am not good at doing, reinforcing the distinction between my *wants* and my *shoulds*. I do not particularly like administrative activities. I like making decisions, and I am good at making decisions, but I am not a strong researcher. Others seemed to agree: When I asked for feedback about my Unique Ability®, not a single person said "organizational" or "research" skills were my forte.[2] With

---

2. As you read through these chapters, note that you might have an epiphany that relates to an earlier assignment. For instance, if pondering your Unique Ability® reminds you of activities you should add to your Pyramid Flip™, feel free to go back and update Your Life by Design™ worksheets, extra copies of which can be downloaded at **WWW.CURTISESTES.BIZ.**

this information, I was validated and more free to say "no" to those activities that fell outside my Unique Ability®, instead allowing someone who was more capable and enthusiastic about performing those activities.

I am often asked this question: "What if I love doing something, but I am not good at it?" My response is that you have a couple of options. First, you can and should develop hobbies. I have a dear friend and superstar, Philip Tirone, who, though he is good at many things, cannot carry a beat. Yet he keeps taking dance lessons as a hobby because he loves to dance. Of course, Philip could try to turn this passion into a career, as can you (your second option). Philip could walk away from his thriving business and start auditioning for music videos. However, I strongly doubt his ability to land a single gig.

Like Philip, I am certain you have many things you like to do. Reading *Unique Ability*® and/or joining Strategic Coach® (**WWW.STRATEGICCOACH.COM**) will help you distinguish between those things you like doing and at which you also excel, and other activities you simply enjoy. By focusing on the former for your vocation and the latter as your hobbies, you can find a happy balance.

As part of my discovery process, I also took the Kolbe Index, a 36-item questionnaire intended to tell a person how he "ticks." Unlike an IQ test, which tells you what you can do, or a personality test, which tells you what you want to do, the Kolbe Index will tell you what you will or will not do by measuring your natural instincts. In determining a vision and defining a person's unique ability, the Kolbe Index can be invaluable. Another valuable tool is Marcus Buckingham's book, *Now Discover Your Strengths*. His "Strengthfinder" test will help you clarify where you should be spending your time for maximum results. Visit **WWW.KOLBE.COM** and **WWW.MARCUSBUCKINGHAM.COM** for more information.

VISION-BUILDING ACTIVITY #4

—The To Be List™

The tragedy of life is not in the fact of death, but in what dies inside of you while you live.
—Norman Cousins

WE HAVE ALL USED "TO DO" LISTS AS A MEANS OF TRACKING THINGS that need to get done. However, they are nothing more than trans*actional* documents for crossing chores off the list. I want you to experience a quantum leap by creating a trans*formational* document, your To Be List™. Using the previous activities as the foundation, begin crafting your To Be List™ to identify who you want to be in your life. This is a byproduct of all previous activities, establishing who you want to be as the driving force of everything else. For example, in Activity #1, I identified "Recommitting my life to Christ" as one of my greatest moments in life. In Activity #2, one of my penthouse activities was "Memorizing Philippians for the Bible." In Activity #3, when I asked for feedback on my Unique Ability®, six of my respondents commented on my Christian faith. From this, I can draw a connection to an obvious aspiration of mine: I want to be a man of God, the first item on my To Be List™.

Curtis Estes's To Be List

- To be a man of God.
- To be an adoring husband, always treating my wife better than I would my best client.
- To be a devoted father, eager to play on the floor at my children's level.
- To be a student of culture and history.
- To be generous at every occasion, anonymously if possible.
- To serve others, especially when I get nothing in return.
- To be a champion of education, providing many scholarships for those in need.
- To be thankful for my many blessings and hold onto material possessions loosely.
- To be contagiously joy-filled, promoting optimism and encouragement.
- To be humble and directly credit God as the source of my strength.
- To be patriotic, supporting our country and placing my hand over my heart during the National Anthem.
- To be glad to pick up trash and keep our communities beautiful.
- To be an advocate for others in creating their bigger futures.

Using Activity #1 through Activity #3 as inspiration, create a bulleted list of phrases that describe who you want to be. Consider the answers to these questions:

- *What do I want people to say about me when I am not in the room?*

- *What do I want my spouse and children to think?*

- *What kind of personal brand do I want to have?*

- *In what ways do I want to embrace life?*

- *What are the qualities that are most important to me?*

- *What hobbies that bring me joy, peace, or inspiration do I want to pursue?*

- *How do I want to grow spiritually?*

- *Where can I serve others and make an extraordinary impact?*

- *What do I want my approach to health and fitness to be?*

- *Imagine I am voted* Person of the Year. *Why? What did I achieve to earn this recognition?*

Considering the answers to these questions, fill in your To Be List™ in the space provided below.

TO BE LIST™

_____

_____

_____

_____

_____

_____

_____

_____

_____

_____

_____

_____

_____

_____

_____

_____

_____

_____

_____

VISION-BUILDING ACTIVITY #5

—Your Personal Legacy™

> *Life should not be a journey to the grave with the intention of arriving*
> *safely in an attractive and well preserved body, but rather to skid in*
> *sideways, champagne in one hand, strawberries in the other, totally*
> *worn out and screaming, "WOO HOO! What a ride!"*
>
> —UNKNOWN

WHO DO YOU WANT TO BE? This is the question that the vision answers, and Activity #4, the To Be List™, spoke to the crux of this question. Activity #5 now builds on this by delving deep into the layers of your ideal self by asking you to outline the legacy you want to leave. This exercise is intended to provide insight into avoiding the great tragedy of the person who meets the end of life with the heavy burden of regret and longing. By writing your own legacy now, years before the end of your life, you can identify who you want to be and take the reigns to steer toward a life you design. This exercise will help you achieve greater clarity about your vision, having already identified those activities you like and dislike (Activity #2), considered your Unique Ability® (Activity #3), and brainstormed for who you want to be (Activity #4). At the end of Activity #5, you will prioritize and synthesize what you want people to say about you, which will allow you to create a direction as to who you must be so that you can fulfill this legacy.

Imagine the day, years from now, when your dearest loved ones, family and friends are gathered together to celebrate and honor your life. If you could craft the words on their hearts, what would they say? How would you be remembered? What mark will you have left behind? What are they saying about you? Will they say you were generous, loving, bold, gentle, kind, brave, and patient? Or will they be forced to speak euphemisms because, in fact, you were a hurried, self-absorbed workaholic?

A legacy-making hero of mine is the Fox News anchor Bret Baier, who consistently rises to the challenge in any setting. In his recent book, *Special Heart*, Bret shares, "The dividing line between success and failure for a project is simply one person stepping in to fill the gap and putting themselves in the uncomfortable position of speaking up or even taking charge, if that is what is required."

Bret has exemplified this throughout his life, from being a random volunteer at a soup kitchen who ends up leading the effort to serve Thanksgiving dinner for the homeless on the Capital Lawn, to reporting and highlighting the bravery of our troops from the front lines in Afghanistan, to transforming the fundraising for Children's National Medical Center raising more than $10 million dollars in a single night. I recently had lunch with Bret, and we brainstormed bringing the Suitcase Party to D.C. Wouldn't it be fun to see if we could raise $12 million next year?

Here is my personal legacy and it drives me to live my life to the utmost.

Personal Legacy of Curtis Estes

"Forgetting what is behind and straining toward what is ahead, I press on toward the goal to win the prize for which God called me heavenward in Jesus Christ," Philippians 3:13-14. This was Curtis Estes's spiritual mission, and he fulfilled it. Through fire and trials, he sustained and lived a life of integrity, commitment, truth, and love. Before the blessing of his most precious family, Curtis found and honored his beloved lifetime relationship with Jesus Christ. All efforts and direction in his life were aligned with the burning passion of this relationship. Curtis represented a true man of God.

He was compassionate, bold, open, and ever-present in the lives of those he loved and touched. Curtis responded to need with attention and action. He supported and celebrated the community. His commitment to the education of children emanates from the desks and walls of the Bel Air Presbyterian Elementary School, a place that has fostered the education and brightly shining futures of countless children. His efforts stretched beyond his community and into the betterment of the world. This is evidenced by the creation and success of The Polhemus Hall for Inspired Leadership at Whitworth University, a place that continues to nurture some of the country's finest future leaders. To date, the Curtis and Kristi Estes Family Foundation has contributed $100 million to enrich and sustain families in need as well as lift the human spirit. Yet, his most significant contribution to this life is reflected in the eyes of his wife, children, grandchildren, and dear friends. His reflection of service above self, Christian values, loyalty, contribution, joy, and steadfast love abounds in his legacy.

Using my legacy as an example, consider what you want others to say about you. When writing your legacy, be sure to examine your character, goals, achievements, contributions, and values. Do not write the legacy of the person you are today but rather of the person you are going to be tomorrow, drawing from your To Be List™ for inspiration. Write your legacy on the following page.

Your Personal Legacy™

_____
_____
_____
_____
_____
_____
_____
_____
_____
_____
_____
_____
_____
_____
_____
_____
_____
_____
_____
_____
_____
_____
_____
_____
_____
_____
_____
_____
_____
_____
_____
_____

VISION-BUILDING ACTIVITY #6

—Creating The Bigger Vision™

> *Do not ask yourself what the world needs; ask yourself what makes*
> *you come alive. And then go and do that. Because, what the world*
> *needs is more people who have come alive.*
> —Harold Whitman

UNTIL NOW, YOUR LIFE BY DESIGN™ HAS FOCUSED ON BRAINSTORMING activities that spark thought as to your vision and cause you to take deep inventory of your life. Now it is time to draft your vision, which will be the springboard to creating your strategy. Keep in mind that:

- Your vision should be written in the present tense. Act as though you are already living your vision. Act as if you are already "the new you" today instead of wishing to be that person tomorrow. For instance, instead of writing: "My vision is to be a man of God," write: "I am a man of God." Likewise, "My vision is to spend more time with my family" is not as strong as a vision that reads, "I am a family man." By stating your vision in the present tense, your subconscious mind will begin to embrace your vision, and you will be more likely to take action that supports this vision and brings it into reality.

- Your vision should be positive, inspiring, and personal. One of my colleagues has the following vision: "I chew on nails for breakfast, and then I have a cocktail." To me, this vision sounds like gibberish; to her, it is deeply personal and inspiring.

  I asked her once what her vision means: "When I was a kid, my dad, who loves the book *The Great Santini*, always boasted that his kids 'can chew on nails while other kids suck on cotton candy,'" she said. "It is a quote from the book, and it reminds me to be disciplined, to hit the ground running. But I have a tendency to become too disciplined, so I need a vision that reminds me to have fun as well. After a full day of work, I wind down and relax with a glass of wine or a movie with my husband, friends, and family," she explained.

  My point? While the vision didn't make sense to me, it was perfect for my colleague. Yours, too, should be something that touches you and moves you to action.

- Your vision can be as long or as short, as specific or as vague, as to fit your needs. Some coaches and strategists suggest that a vision be just one sentence long and that it be an overarching vision that speaks to each aspect of a person's life. For the purpose of *Your Life by Design™*, feel free to throw this concept out the window and create a vision that works for you. It could be as simple and broad as "I am a man of God," or as complex and detailed as mine, which follows:

  > **Curtis Estes's Vision:** I have great health so that I can thrive to age 132. I am surrounded with people I care deeply about and who are committed to mutual growth and joy. I live from a position of financial strength while being generous on every occasion. I serve my valued clients as a Strategic Breakthrough Partner and strive to delight them at every interaction. I have great people

frequently saying great things about me to other great people. I help others give success true meaning. I fill my weeks with great memory-making experiences. Daily I conform my life to Christ so that I can be my best and serve the most as I seek to fulfill my most amazing future sooner than anyone expects.

- Your vision can and will be modified. As we move through this process, you will begin seeing life with a fresh perspective. Feel free to change and modify your vision accordingly!

- You should post your vision in a place that reminds you each day of its significance. My dear friend, Philip Tirone, printed a nightshirt with his vision written in reverse. Each morning when he awakes, the first thing he does is brush his teeth, staring at his vision in the mirror; each evening, he repeats this activity, reminding himself of his vision. If this is too radical for you, try programming your screen saver as your vision or beginning and ending each day by rewriting your vision.

For now, carefully craft your vision:

As you build your vision, think about those people who are closest to you. How might these ideas be helpful to them? Share these exercises and encourage your friends, colleagues, and family members to create their own bigger futures. Learn more at our website, www.curtisestes.biz, where you can find additional vision-building activities, such as the Lifetime Dream List™ and the Best Day Ever exercises.

COACHING TIP:
Position your day for success by re-writing your vision each morning. In this way, you put your vision in the forefront of your mind, pointing your life in the direction of your design. Or if you prefer, read it or have it be read to you by the fabulous free smart phone app Natural Reader.

Rewrite your vision each morning:

_____
_____
_____
_____
_____
_____
_____
_____
_____
_____
_____
_____
_____
_____
_____
_____
_____
_____
_____
_____
_____
_____
_____
_____
_____
_____
_____
_____
_____
_____
_____
_____
_____
_____
_____
_____
_____

THE FIVE COMPONENTS FOR CREATING YOUR STRATEGY

BIGGER VISION

SPECIFIC STRATEGY DRIVEN BY THE COMPELLING *WHY*

EXACTING IMPLEMENTATION

TRANSFORMING RESULTS

THE FIVE COMPONENTS FOR CREATING YOUR STRATEGY

It is a paradoxical but profoundly true and important principle of life
that the most likely way to reach a goal is to be aiming not at that
goal itself but at some more ambitious goal beyond it.
—Arnold Toynbee

LIFE IS NOTHING MORE THAN A SERIES OF MOMENTS; or rather, it is nothing *less*. A life is significant when it is filled with positive moments that intentionally move a person toward his vision; a life filled with negative or meaningless moments leaves a person feeling unfulfilled. A good friend once told me that at the end of the day, we will appreciate the memories more than the money. In other words, the moments that comprise our life are more significant than all the success in the world. No more direct road to personal satisfaction and fulfillment of dreams exists than the one paved with strategy—the goals that will fill our lives with meaningful moments.

Goals represent beacons that help us navigate the twists and turns, discoveries, and events that comprise these moments, reminding us of and leading us to our ultimate vision. Goals clarify the opportunity within each of these moments, defining what these moments will look like, and whether they will be positive and productive or negative and insignificant. They direct the actions a person takes.

Recognizing that goals exist to move us to positive and desirable action, the question then becomes: What should my goals look like? I imagine goals as a point of tension on a rubber band. We must stretch to achieve them. This stretch is what supports our progress, and therefore, it must be aggressive, but not so aggressive that it becomes counterproductive, snapping the rubber band. Perhaps you saw the humorous Japanese commercial of the man who was competing in a tree-catching contest. As his teammates swing their axes at the base of the tree, the man positions himself to catch the giant tree. Of course, the tree falls and lands on top of him, flattening him to the ground. Compare this to Paul Potts, the Welsh mobile phone salesman who dreamed of being an opera star. Seemingly against all odds, Potts auditioned for *Britain's Got Talent*, a televised talent show that debuted in 2007. Singing opera in a modern talent show, Potts was already at a disadvantage, and his obstacles magnified as he stood before Simon Cowell, a ruthless and unforgiving judge. But Potts brought the audience to their feet, moving more than a few listeners to tears, and breaking through Cowell's callous tendencies. The judges deemed Potts to be a diamond-in-the-making. Potts was not only sent through to the next round, and the next, but he also won the entire competition. And the cherry on top of the ice cream? The first album Potts released ranked first on the UK Album Chart.

The moral of the stories? Our goals should push us past our current point of comfort to a point that is ambitious, but the goal must be possible; it should not flatten us along the way. We should then use these big overarching goals as tools to grow our current capabilities. Just because you do not have the current ability to reach an audacious goal does not mean you should not aim for it. Think of all the skills, relationships, and opportunities that have come to you over the last 10 years. If your goals were based on who you were 10 years ago instead of who you have become, you would not be nearly as successful as you are today.

Bookstores are overflowing with resources that describe the process of setting goals. But the truth is that proper goal setting can be boiled down to five rules:

1. The goals must be tied to an emotionally compelling *why* aligned with your vision (Strategy Component #1—The Compelling *Why* Catalyst™).

2. The goals must be SMART (Strategy Component #2—The SMART Goals Formula™).

3. The goals must be balanced and integrated (Strategy Component #3—Achieving Balance and Integration with the SMART Goals Action Plan™).

4. The goals must be linked to a reward or consequence that drives you to completion (Strategy Component #4—The Rewards and Consequences Multiplier™).

5. The goals must move you toward your ideal day (Strategy Component #5—Designing Your Ideal Day™).

STRATEGY COMPONENT #1

—The Compelling *Why* Catalyst™

Of all the sad words of tongue and pen, the saddest of all are these:
"It might have been."
> —JOHN GREENLEAF WHITTIER

THE MAJORITY OF SUPERSTARS ARE ALREADY WELL SCHOOLED in the fundamentals and importance of goal setting or they would not be so successful. Yet though they are master strategists, too many lack goals that are aligned with a vision integrating each area of life necessary for fulfillment. Often, their success is based on their ability to make snap decisions, to pull the trigger and take action. Though these qualities are admirable, they must be kept in check lest we risk living by default, taking convenient or artificial steps instead of significant and intentional steps. These highly talented people sometimes fail to reach fulfillment because they set and implement inappropriate goals, albeit with brilliant efficacy, especially when they do not have an emotionally compelling *why* that drives their actions.

Let's consider the story of the two bricklayers. A passerby notices the first bricklayer laboring in the hot afternoon sun. He looks miserable and worn.

"Whatever are you doing in this hot afternoon sun?" asks the passerby.

"What does it look like? I am laying bricks," snarls the first bricklayer.

Around the corner, the passerby meets another bricklayer, this one whistling with a smile while working on a different wall of the same project.

"Whatever are you doing in this hot afternoon sun?" asks the passerby.

"Oh, sir," he says with an air of great importance, "*I* am building a cathedral."

With a big enough *why*, any activity can be meaningful and motivating. But if you do not have a compelling *why*, you are merely laying bricks. The *why* anchors the activity to the desired outcome. For instance, I want to keep meetings with five great clients a day (the activity) so that I can build my business (the goal). Why? So that Kristi and I can travel more, spending a full month each year living in another country raising our children as global citizens (the ultimate desired outcome).

Goals are not meant to merely assign a quantitative measure to achievements, but rather to provide the fuel necessary to sustain the motivational fire. The task of continuously stoking the fire is a mighty one that separates those who are thriving from those who are only surviving. Those who constantly revisit their goals, altering them so as to better support their vision and keep them aligned with their core values, are more likely to describe themselves as successful than those who do not. If a person sets a goal of generating $200,000 of additional income in three months, the pursuit of this goal might require him to spend less time with his family, one of his core values. As such, he is sabotaging his own happiness by causing the moments of his day to be incongruent with his values and vision.

In 2004 as I stepped aboard a plane, I realized I was guilty of living with goals that no longer held as much priority in my life. Prior to the birth of my first child, Jordan, I traveled extensively. On top of my other professional commitments, I spent two days each month leading coaching seminars, the proceeds of which I donated to charity. When I was single, and then when I was married with no children, these speaking events held deep meaning for me. I was raising $2,500 per day and donating $60,000 annually.

I recognized that each day I spent away from Jordan, I missed his development. I knew that the first three years of a child's life are critically important, and I was traveling so often that I was missing his life. Yes, I was raising money for a good cause, but I was doing so at the expense of my child. This was not a sacrifice I wanted to make.

I realized I was living by default in this area of my life. Though my goal of raising money for charity had been a good one, the strategy was outdated, and it did not support my other goals, or my revised vision of being an outstanding father. Then and there, I made a commitment: I would stop traveling so often. I revamped my goals related to the coaching seminars so that instead of traveling once a month, I would travel only four times per year, providing private coaching sessions instead of public speaking events.

I have often said that a byproduct of leading a significant, meaningful life is financial success. An interesting thing happens when we step back and tend to other areas of our lives: We feel more at peace, and we are more energized in all areas of life. As a result, we experience positive changes in all aspects and sometimes benefit from amazing strategic byproducts. Consider what happened when I stopped traveling monthly and delivering the seminars. I got creative and replaced this activity with a quarterly trip whereby I privately coached 10 individuals. Instead of making $2,500 each day, I started raising $10,000 each day. I quadrupled my productivity while reducing my professional commitment. In other words, by reevaluating my professional life and favoring my personal life, I positively affected both! How did this happen? I believe, and countless philosophers and psychologists agree, that a well-integrated life is a more productive life and that the world will respond positively to those living in congruence with their vision and values. I believe that we are attracted to people who are shining examples, and that we respond positively to those who set goals that are integrated with their vision and values.

STRATEGY COMPONENT #2

—The SMART Goals Formula™

Some people regard discipline as a chore. For me, it is a kind of order that sets me free to fly.
—Julie Andrews

BEING SMART ABOUT GOALS MEANS YOU HAVE TAKEN THE TIME to strategically craft the activities that lead to fulfillment of a goal, making these goals guided, supported, and achievable. The SMART system ensures that your goals are: **Specific, Measurable, Action-oriented, Results-oriented,** and **Time-bound**. As you apply these guidelines to your goals, you will have quantifiable measures to keep yourself accountable and ultimately serve you in attaining your vision.

Specific—Be as specific as possible when crafting goals. Vagueness is like kryptonite to goals—an unseen force that weakens and destroys. When steps to achieving goals are written in precise, detailed, and clear language, the subconscious mind, which actualizes goals, engages and harnesses its energy to accomplish the task at hand. If used properly, the subconscious mind can be a powerful ally. Questions to consider that will ensure you have been specific include: Who? What? When? Where? How? For example, if your goal is to achieve your best health, the specific action necessary to qualify this as a SMART goal might be: To run four times weekly starting immediately and building up to a 45-minute 10K.

Measurable—Establish systems by which you can accurately track the progress you have made toward attaining your goals. Measuring your progress serves as a motivational tool, as well as promoting accountability, and the rewarding feeling of achievement. To ensure that goals are measurable, ask yourself: When will this be accomplished? By how much? By how many? Remember: What you measure, matters.

One of my visions is to strengthen my reputation as a man of Christ. As stated, however, this is not particularly measurable. How can I determine whether I am working toward this vision without measurable goals that support it? Therefore, the SMART goal that supports this vision is to spend at least 15 minutes each day studying the Bible.

Action-oriented—One of the key differences between a goal and a vision is the action tied to the goal. The best goals are those that require growth and motion. After all, no personal growth begins until we start moving. Once you have set actionable goals, you will be moving along the path toward your vision. For instance, if your vision is "to achieve great health," you have not defined a strategy or action plan to move toward this vision. This is where goals come into play. Actionable means that you are taking steps, even if they are small, toward your vision.

Results-oriented—Does your goal support your vision? Is it tied to a specified result? Your goal must be on a throughline from where you are today to your ideal life. How is the goal relevant to the end result? Goals must be important to you in the grand scheme of things. If the result does not inspire you, choose a different goal or you will be unlikely to take steps to move the goal forward.

Time-bound—Every goal must be grounded within a determined timeframe. Without a timeframe there is no sense of urgency. If you want to run a 10K, when is the race? Planning on "someday" will surely weaken your efforts. Ground your goals with activities that fit within a specific timeframe, and you will increase the likelihood for success exponentially.

To make sure your goals are SMART, use the following worksheet. Start by considering just one goal, then refer back to this worksheet anytime you need help ironing out the specifics of additional goals. (Remember to download additional worksheets at **WWW.CURTISESTES.BIZ**.)

SMART Goals Worksheet™

Goal: _____

_____

_____

_____

What will you do? What specifically is your goal? Provide as many details as possible. _____

_____

_____

_____

_____

_____

How will you measure or evaluate achievement of the goal? _____

_____

_____

_____

_____

_____

What is your first action step? What are the successive steps? What do you need to change or stop doing? _____

_____

_____

_____

_____

_____

_____

How is this goal related to your vision? What is the emotionally compelling why? What will the result be? _____

_____

_____

_____

_____

When will you achieve the goal? _____

_____

STRATEGY COMPONENT #3

—Achieving Balance and Integration with the SMART Goals Action Plan™

> *This is the true joy in life, the being used for a purpose recognized by yourself as a mighty one; the being a force of nature instead of a feverish, selfish little clod of ailments and grievances complaining that the world will not devote itself to making you happy. I am of the opinion that my life belongs to the whole community, and as long as I live it is my privilege to do for it whatever I can. I want to be thoroughly used up when I die, for the harder I work the more I live. I rejoice in life for its own sake. Life is no 'brief candle' for me. It is a sort of splendid torch which I have got hold of for the moment, and I want to make it burn as brightly as possible before handing it on to future generations.*
>
> —GEORGE BERNARD SHAW

OVERACHIEVERS ARE OFTEN GUILTY of investing their heart and soul into one or two areas of life, leaving the remaining areas malnourished. Inherent in *Your Life by Design™* is the concept of integration. Similar to the concept of balance, integration means that you are focusing on each aspect of your life. However, unlike people who strive for balance alone, which often means that they compartmentalize different areas of life and dedicate time to each separate component, those who strive for integration set goals that integrate the entirety of their vision. If I strive to be a man of God, I must have a profession that allows me to support this. In my profession I have great flexibility to be a family man, another component of my vision. I consider each aspect of my life when setting a goal so that I have balance among all aspects of my life. I would not accept a job that affected my relationship with God or with my family members. I would not accept a profession that kept me tied to a desk, even if I spent a great deal of time balancing my extroverted nature by socializing while I was away from work. Though I might achieve balance this way, I would not be integrating all of my values when considering a goal or path.

For me, success represents the confluence of work and play, the presence of a vision in each goal so that activities and life become significant, not just successful.

To make sure that I achieve this integration, I have established eight categories that cover every significant life area. I set a vision (and corresponding SMART goals) in each category using the SMART Goals Action Plan™. As you can see from the sample of my SMART Goals Action Plan™, within each category I ask myself whether these goals support my overall vision, making sure that I am taking significant steps that tie my behavior (goals) back into my vision.

The eight goal categories are:

1. Health

2. Relationships

3. Financial

4. Professional Growth

5. Reputation

6. Community Contribution

7. Fun and Hobbies

8. Personal and Spiritual Growth

Curtis Estes's SMART Goals Action Plan™

Overall Health Vision: To have great health that lasts a lifetime.

a. Exercise in some fashion every single day, inviting friends to join me in Olympic distance triathlons the first Friday of each month.

b. Track my trail-run intervals using the Garmin to go sub-38, beating my best time of 38:13. Complete 20 quarter-mile sprints at 8.8 on the Woodway.

c. Implement Robert Cooper's Apex Operating System with my Miracle Morning regimen of pushups in bright light, followed by breathing fresh morning air and envisioning my most emotionally compelling five-year goals while looking at the horizon starting July 1.

Compelling *why*: So that I can be running races and chasing great-grandchildren at age 132.

Overall Relationship Vision: To surround myself with people I care deeply about and who are committed to mutual growth and joy.

a. Enjoy a weekly date night with my wife and have candlelight dinners at home starting August 1.

b. Pray with the kids throughout the day for the concerns we see like racing ambulances and homeless people beginning now.

c. Play during Friday Family Fun Nights to make joy a hallmark of our time together and Sunday Family Meetings to intentionally grow together beginning September 1.

Compelling *why*: So that I continue to have the marriage I dreamed of and raise children who become adults I admire.

Overall Financial Vision: To live from a position of financial strength.

a. Invest an additional $25,000 every quarter into permanent life insurance starting October 1.

b. Update our Freedom Plan every month toward attaining our 100% Freedom Ratio (thanks to Dave Fenton) starting January 1.

c. Implement Estes Giving Plan making transformational gifts in amounts equaling as much as we save by December 15 (ultimately increasing giving to 50 percent of personal income).

Compelling *why*: So that I never have to work by my children's side at McDonald's and, more importantly, so that I can be generous on every occasion.

Overall Professional Growth Vision: To serve my valued clients as a strategic breakthrough partner.

    a. Practice Ideal Partnership focus with Juan Baron so that we are each leveraging our Unique Ability® for exponential growth beginning July 1.

    b. Hire mobile marketing assistant/ideal life facilitator so that I can reclaim all drive time for productivity and stay wholly focused on my most important priorities without being distracted by "stuff" by September 5.

    c. Implement program to delight our clients at every interaction beginning October 1.

Compelling *why*: By delighting my clients at every interaction, I will have more fun, enjoy bigger rewards, and eliminate the competition.

Overall Reputation Vision: To have great people frequently say great things about me to other great people.

    a. As a result of delighting our clients at every interaction, our clients are giving us referrals to 20 friends monthly as of August 1.

    b. Become dramatically more interesting by paying exceptional attention to all those with whom I interact, to be initiated by identifying their eye color, beginning now.

    c. Identify and cultivate our Recommenders so that we are appropriately recognizing and serving them as the true growth multipliers of our practice.

Compelling *why*: So that I can continually be growing my practice, while always meeting, befriending and connecting superstars for mutual benefit.

Overall Community Contribution Vision: To help others in need, as I have been blessed to be a blessing.

    a. As campaign co-chair, help Pacifica Christian High School raise $5 million to launch our new middle school beginning January 1.

    b. Ask my family the following question during dinner: "What did we do today to make someone's life better?" beginning October 1.

c. Teach my children to always say, "please," "thank you," and "you are welcome" by modeling this behavior and encouraging them daily beginning immediately.

d. Start the National Center for Fathering (www.FATHERS.COM) Watch D.O.G's (Dads of Great Students) program at Bel Air Presbyterian Preschool on September 1.

Compelling *why*: So that I can know that I have touched the hearts of people, many of whom I will never meet.

Overall Fun and Hobbies Vision: To fill my weeks with great memory-making experiences.

a. Actively participate in Reasner, Adkinson and Pettit book club to sharpen my critical thinking and broaden my literary depth and appreciation beginning August 1.

b. Weekly bicycling and beach/trail runs with friends beginning September 1.

c. Dinner (followed by dancing) with my wife and friends at the top seven highest-rated Zagat restaurants to be completed by December 31.

d. Quarterly "staycation" vacation at home to enjoy our great city beginning July 1. Each year spend an additional week enjoying global citizenship travel with the family.

Compelling *why*: So that I can maintain the skip in my step that makes waking up so much more enjoyable.

Overall Personal and Spiritual Growth Vision: To daily conform my life to Christ.

a. Start every morning with reading *Jesus Calling*, the *One Year Bible*, journaling my application for the verse that speaks to me the most and learning deeply in the Classroom of Silence beginning now.

b. Use Natural Reader to listen to my Lifebook Premise, Vision, Purpose and Strategies in all 12 areas of life as soon as I get in the car each morning beginning now.

c. Monthly confession with my pastor starting October 1.

d. Begin quarterly family mission trips, starting with serving the families at Harvest Home beginning September 1.

Compelling *why*: So that I can become the best version of myself and serve the most.

My SMART Goals Action Plan™ is among the worksheets I update the most often. Indeed, I update this worksheet weekly, making sure that my goals shift in tandem with life's changes and my accomplishments.[1]

COACHING TIP:

Write down everything you think you need in order to feel happy and successful. Then identify the ones you feel totally committed to making come true. You can probably narrow this list to only four or five things you must do to die without regret. Now create a plan to act on the first one by sundown on Sunday.

These eight areas of life are not listed in order of priority, as they all hold significant value. However, the level of importance that a person is placing (consciously or otherwise) on each category is gauged by the types of goals that are set within each category. By differentiating these categories, a person forces herself to pay attention to a category she might have otherwise been neglecting.

Fair attention is needed in all areas if our lives are to truly flourish. True success and fulfillment must be measured from a perspective that encompasses all areas of life. Seeking balance in life takes concerted effort and steadfast attention. There are no shortcuts. Defining the important areas of your life lessens the risk that you might overlook them.

Keeping in mind that *Your Life by Design™* considers every aspect of life, spend time setting the overall vision in each area of your life you deem significant to achieve balance and integration. Then, using the SMART Goals Action Plan™ Worksheet, set at least three goals that support your broader vision. Remember to use the SMART goals criteria when setting each step.

This worksheet will be the document you will refer to, be held accountable to, and update most often.

---

1. For a current version of my SMART Goals Action Plan™, visit WWW.CURTISESTES.BIZ. There, you can update your personal SMART Goals Action Plan™ and view the worksheets of others in the Your Life by Design® community.

The SMART Goals Action Plan™ Worksheet

Overall Health Vision: _____

Specific SMART Goals
a. _____

b. _____

c. _____

Compelling *why*: _____

_____

Overall Relationship Vision: _____

Specific SMART Goals
a. _____

b. _____

c. _____

Compelling *why*: _____

_____

Overall Financial Vision: _____

_____

Specific SMART Goals

a. _____

b. _____

c. _____

Compelling *why*: _____

_____

Overall Professional Vision: _____

_____

Specific SMART Goals

a. _____

b. _____

c. _____

Compelling *why*: _____

_____

Overall Reputation Vision: _____

Specific SMART Goals

a. _____

b. _____

c. _____

Compelling *why*: _____

_____

Overall Community Contribution Vision: _____

Specific SMART Goals

a. _____

b. _____

c. _____

Compelling *why*: _____

_____

Overall Fun and Hobbies Vision: _____

Specific SMART Goals

a. _____

b. _____

c. _____

Compelling *why*: _____

Overall Personal and Spiritual Vision: _____

Specific SMART Goals

a. _____

b. _____

c. _____

Compelling *why*: _____

COACHING TIP:

It is crucial to have both short-term and long-term goals. As you define goals for each area of your life, identify whether it is a 30-day goal, or a three-year goal. Perhaps you want to create a different Goal Action Plan Worksheet™ for immediate, midrange, and long-term goals. Visit www. CURTISESTES.BIZ to find goal templates for your different time horizons.

STRATEGY COMPONENT #4

—The Rewards and Consequences Multiplier™

Only those who risk going too far can possibly find out how far one can go.
　　　　　　—T.S. Eliot

ONE OF THE MORE EFFECTIVE STRATEGIES FOR HOLDING yourself accountable is through the power of rewards and consequences, by either setting up penalties that move you away from what you do not want in life or rewards that move you toward it. For instance, if your goal is to spend more time on your health and fitness, implement a system that ensures that you do this. A client of mine has committed to five days per week of exercise. To keep her on track, she joined a small, private gym and asked the owner to keep her accountable: If she does not attend five days per week, her credit card is charged $200 for each day missed. Because of this, she has not missed one day and is well on her way toward reaching her goal.

Others find the pursuit of pleasure a better source of motivation. These individuals prefer taking actions that move them *toward* what they want in life. For example, if such a person wanted to lose weight or achieve physical fitness, she might stay motivated by anticipating a trip she has planned to Hawaii where she will celebrate her newfound shape and fitness. *If I exercise five days a week, I will treat myself and my husband to a trip to Hawaii*, she tells herself.

Another method of establishing accountability is to "go public." Going public means you have declared your goals to individuals whom you admire and respect, and the thought of publicly failing compels you to action. According to Cooper, "When you make a verbal commitment to another person—or to yourself in the mirror, eye to eye, you are as much as 70 percent more likely to take the actions that honor that commitment."[2] Consider Erik Flexner, a superstar in the real estate arena. Erik has achieved excellence in most areas of his life, and he has maintained his standing as the top realtor in his company for several years. He has defied industry trends and continued to consistently grow his business despite a significant downward turn in the California real estate market. Even with great professional commitments, he has been able to achieve balance in other areas of his life. His life is not solely about business and he has a flourishing personal life to prove it: a wife, a son, and a large group of friends.

But in the past, when Erik's life became hectic, he would drop his fitness routine. While planning for his wedding, Erik found himself unable to maintain the level of fitness he desired. With a romantic honeymoon in Brazil just four short months away, Erik set a goal to lose twenty pounds before his trip. He set this personal goal not just on paper but also in a declaration to his entire professional networking group, a close-knit group that had become friends in addition to networking colleagues. He admitted his plan and then vowed to stand defeated and shirtless in front of everyone in the group should he not reach the goal.

Erik needed only to lose five pounds per month, and the penalty for failure horrified him, so he scheduled time in his calendar to avoid this humiliating experience, working out regularly and changing his diet to accommodate his new weight goal. He achieved his goal, kept his clothes on, escaped public defeat, and enjoyed his honeymoon with his beautiful wife by his side.

The moral of the story is to find out what method best sparks you to take action, light the match, and watch the blaze. One way or another, keeping oneself accountable to one's goals, and setting high rewards or penalties for failing to participate in the activities that drive these goals, is critical to *Your Life by Design™*.

---

2. R. B. Cialdini, *Influence, The Psychology of Persuasion* (New York: Quill, 1993).

Going public also provides a "buy in" from your support team, including family and friends. A husband who tells his wife he wants to start exercising to stop heart problems gives his wife an opportunity to join him or help him. A person who goes public at work can create a health challenge for the entire office so co-workers stop bringing candy into the office.

For some of us, resistance to change seems inescapable. Settling back into old habits and resisting seems to be part of our human condition. If we cannot escape this, we must seek creative ways to cope with it and fight it. Invoking change is entirely possible but at times, it takes more than self-control and will. Experiencing lasting change in life takes strategy and consistency. In business, we are held accountable by our bosses, our clients, or our employees. The consequences of not taking action can be devastating, and the rewards can be life-changing. In life, we must create structures that mirror these same penalties and rewards, which is where going public with your Personal Board of Advisors™ can come into play, as we will discuss in Implementation Tactic #2—The Personal Board of Advisors™. By telling your board members, your spouse, or even your children how to hold you accountable, you will successfully create structures that are natural within businesses, thereby setting into motion *Your Life by Design™*.

The following are a few examples of my goals with corresponding self-imposed accountability and rewards/consequences.

Curtis Estes's Rewards and Consequences Multiplier™

Goal: To get really comfortable swimming one mile in the ocean and complete the Malibu triathlon.

Accountability: Declared goal to my Personal Board of Advisors™ and running partner, Sean Burton.

Consequence: I will treat Sean to a bottle of his favorite wine, Opus One, if I do not meet my goal of competing in the Malibu triathlon.

Goal: To save an additional $25,000 each quarter beginning next quarter.

Accountability: Declared goal to my personal Board of Advisors™ and business manager, Dave Fenton.

Reward: I take my wife out for a special night on the town to celebrate.

Goal: Start a weekly date night with my wife and have candlelight dinners at home starting July 1.

Accountability: Declared goal to my Personal Board of Advisors™ and my wife, Kristi.

Consequence: I do the dishes for each week that I do not keep my most important appointment with my wife.

List each of your goals from the SMART Goals Action Plan™ that began on page 79, and then create an accountability item and reward or consequence in the worksheet below.

Rewards and Penalties Multiplier™

Goal: _____
Accountability: _____
Reward/Consequence: _____

Goal: _____
Accountability: _____
Reward/Consequence: _____

Goal: _____
Accountability: _____
Reward/Consequence: _____

Goal: _____
Accountability: _____
Reward/Consequence: _____

Goal: _____
Accountability: _____
Reward/Consequence: _____

Goal: _____
Accountability: _____
Reward/Consequence: _____

Goal: _____
Accountability: _____
Reward/Consequence: _____

Goal: _____
Accountability: _____
Reward/Consequence: _____

STRATEGY COMPONENT #5

—Designing Your Ideal Day™

A man is known by the books he reads, by the company he keeps, by the praise he gives, by his dress, by his tastes, by his distastes, by the stories he tells, by his gait, by the motion of his eye, by the look of his house, of his chamber; for nothing on Earth is solitary but every thing hath affinities infinite.
—RALPH WALDO EMERSON

UPON DETERMINING YOUR VISION AND SETTING GOALS and activities that support your vision, the next step is to ensure that your schedule supports these goals and activities. Believe it or not, a life that lacks fulfillment and personal satisfaction is often easy to remedy simply by effectively and intentionally using a schedule. People toil away in their day-to-day routines, plagued with confusion as to why they are not happy. All the while, the answer is right before them, hiding within the moments and hours of the day. Look at your schedule, examine how you are spending your time, and ask yourself what actions throughout your day bring you closer to your ultimate vision. Many people spend their entire day taking part in activities and/or responsibilities that bring them little to no pleasure, and then they wonder why they feel so unsatisfied. This is not to say that daily goals and their supporting activities should consist of easy, relaxed, vacation-like behavior, as this would not promote success, productivity, or lasting fulfillment. True fulfillment comes from reaching beyond your current circumstances and becoming more of who you want to be. Creating *Your Life by Design™* requires that you take a proactive approach toward making time for the activities that move you closer to your ideal schedule.

Here, the idea is to create three schedules: the Ideal Schedule, which reflects all the activities that support your vision and underlying goals; the Current Schedule, which is a general snapshot of your current day-to-day activities; and the Daily Schedule, which is recreated each day to denote all of the items on your "to do" list for the upcoming day.

Let's start by considering your Ideal Schedule and how it compares to your Current Schedule. If you could design the perfect day, what would it look like? To be sure, I am not talking about one perfect vacation day, I am talking about your day-to-day schedule—what would your typical day look like ideally? Would you awake eagerly and exercise? Spend time with your children? Read a book? Work six hours instead of 16 hours?

Now, we need to compare this to your Current Schedule. As we have discussed, the importance of your schedule is as important as your goals themselves. Your schedule reflects who you are. Dan Sullivan, founder of the Strategic Coach® says that all progress starts by telling the truth. So, take his advice and make an honest assessment of your Current Schedule. Where are you spending your time? Where are you investing your energy? Compare this Current Schedule to your Pyramid Flip™ and see how much time you are spending in the outhouse as compared to the penthouse.

Current Schedule vs. Ideal Schedule Template™

Current Schedule

6: _____

7: _____

8: _____

9: _____

10: _____

11: _____

12: _____

1: _____

2: _____

3: _____

4: _____

5: _____

6: _____

7: _____

8: _____

Ideal Schedule

6: _____

7: _____

8: _____

9: _____

10: _____

11: _____

12: _____

1: _____

2: _____

3: _____

4: _____

5: _____

6: _____

7: _____

8: _____

Below was my Current Schedule, from the first edition of this book, as compared to my Ideal Schedule.

Curtis's Current Schedule	Curtis's Ideal Schedule
6-7 a.m. Awake and exercise once or twice a week, hit snooze the other days.	**5:30 a.m.** Awake and begin my Miracle Morning regimen of reading, affirmations, exercise and envisioning my most emotionally compelling five-year goals.
8 a.m. Check in with staff at the office.	**6:15 a.m.** Drive to the beach club to complete the rest of my exercise regimen.
9:30 a.m. to 5 p.m. Three or four meetings with clients, with too much driving to appointments and going through busy work that others could be managing. Eating whatever I want throughout the day.	**8 a.m.** Breakfast meeting with a great client.
	9:30 a.m. Check in with the team at the office.
6 p.m. Arrive home to spend time with my family.	**10 a.m. to 4 p.m.** Five more great meetings with clients in my office. Eat a salad at lunch with moderate portions of well-balanced foods throughout the day. Begin last meeting at 3:00 p.m.
6:30 p.m. Dinner as a family.	**5 p.m.** Arrive home to spend time with my family, intentionally "being present" in body and mind.
7:30 p.m. Nightly reading, prayers, and bedtime for kids.	**6:30 p.m.** Healthy dinner as a family.
8 p.m. Watching television and enjoying an evening dessert.	**7:30 p.m.** Nightly reading, prayers, and bedtime for kids.
10 p.m. Pray with my wife on our knees before going to sleep.	**8 p.m.** Reading and/or relaxing with my wife. No evening desserts.
	10 p.m. Pray with my wife on our knees before going to sleep.

Now review your own Current Schedule noting how many hours you spend at work, how many you are with family, and the like, filling in the template on page 91. Then review all the previous exercises in this book, including the penthouse activities, your wants, your vision, your To Be List™, and your SMART goals to determine what you want your Ideal Schedule to look like. Record it in the Ideal Schedule portion of the template. This comparison will give you the framework to see where you can make changes in your Daily Schedule to get where you want to be.

Once you have examined your Current Schedule, its existing energy drains, and satisfaction saboteurs, the ways in which you block your progress will be apparent. You are most likely investing large portions of time and energy participating in activities that simply do not support your life's vision.

The next step is to create a plan to move you toward your Ideal Schedule. Use your day planner to incorporate additional elements of your Ideal Schedule into your Daily Schedule each day. I have no magic formula to offer for creating and shifting to your Ideal Schedule. You simply need to review your vision-building activities and start taking action to create and live by Daily Schedules that begin to shift you toward your Ideal Schedule. To change the direction of your life, you must refocus your energies toward activities that move you in the direction of your Ideal Schedule. You must define and illustrate how that Ideal Schedule looks and feels. Envision it. Smell the crisp morning air of a 6 a.m. run. A heightened level of awareness concerning what you truly seek will determine how you approach your day. How do you want to feel upon rising? How do you want to spend your day? What do you want to feel drifting off to sleep at the end of the day? Define it. Write it down. Speak it.

In creating your Daily Schedule, make sure you eliminate or delegate as many safe house and outhouse activities as possible (see Pyramid Flip™) and replace them with penthouse activities that move you toward your SMART goals. Also, make sure you have scheduled the activities that help you achieve balance and integration. Do not buy into the hype of needing something exotic or sensational to experience lasting change. If you are willing to put in the work, giving as much thought and strategy to your life planning as you do to your business, your life will change. If you are unwilling to put in the work, then it will not.

In the words of Larry Byrd, "I've got a theory that if you give 100 percent all of the time, somehow things will work out in the end."

If investing in your relationship with your spouse and children is important to you, make room in your schedule. Schedule vacations and children's school activities for the year in advance. Book working trips and other activities around that which is most important. If changing your body is something that matters to you, schedule time for exercise.

Think of it this way: If a person wants to speak a new language but does not have a single action in her schedule that supports that goal, what is the likelihood that she will achieve this goal? Remember when I said that a schedule reflects a person's life? I say this because a person's ability to move toward goals is directly influenced by the quality of his or her schedule. Failing to schedule in those activities that would actually allow a person to achieve his goals is the same as living a life by default.

The average Daily Schedule is packed with mundane responsibilities. However, if you are to create the life of your choosing, you must begin the process of removing those activities that do not serve your greater good. Every activity in which you take part is either working toward success, meaning it supports and strengthens those things most valuable to you, or is moving you away from it. If something costs you more than it offers, delegate it to someone else or work to cut it from your life. Any task that has you working in opposition to your vision comes at much too high a cost, and it should either be delegated or removed from your schedule.

> **COACHING TIP:**
>
> *While creating your Ideal Schedule for the workweek should be your first priority, do not miss the opportunity to create a separate Ideal Schedule for the weekend too. As an example, I have a standing Saturday morning appointment with a couple of my friends and their children. We either have breakfast at the "diner" in the basement of the Beverly Hills Hotel or hit the park for fun on the playground.*

Becoming a master of one's schedule seems such a simple task. So simple, in fact, that it is often overlooked. But getting a handle on one's schedule, filling it with *wants* instead of *shoulds* and penthouse activities instead of outhouse activities, is the single most important part of *Your Life by Design™*.

We have talked about how everyone has a To Do List, a transactional list of items that generally consist of errands and duties. I suggest you make a To Not Do List, that helps you create Daily Schedules that move you toward your Ideal Schedule.

A To Not Do List is not a *transactional* list so much as it is another *transformational* list, like the To Be List™. This list will help transform your schedule away from your Current Schedule and toward your Ideal Schedule, the schedule you design.

COACHING TIP:

Living Your Life by Design™ is about placing appropriate value on your precious time. As the conductor of your journey, you are empowered to choose why, where, and how you spend your time. Your time is your single most valuable commodity. One idea to help you prioritize activities is to consider the value of your time, or your hourly rate. While you probably do not get paid by the hour, you can calculate the value of each hour by dividing your annual income by 2,000, which is the typical number of working hours per year. For example, if you earned $500,000 last year, your hourly rate is $250. While this is not an exact science, do not hesitate to pay someone else $20/hour to organize your garage if you can exchange that time for a Saturday afternoon with your family.

The To Not Do List illustrates the actions that are not a good use of your time. This list is derived from your Current Schedule, the Pyramid Flip™, and your list of *wants* and *shoulds*. Your To Not Do List looks not only at the things you want to delegate, but also the things you want to stop doing. It identifies those *shoulds* that do not move you closer to your SMART goals, as well as those things that are a good (but not great) use of your time. For example, if participating in a networking organization is just a good use of your time, you would be better served by replacing it with something that is a great use of your time. If serving on the board of the organization requires a commitment of 10 hours per week, how else could you spend that time? Could you schedule an additional 10 hours per week to spend time with your children? Personally, I would like to spend far less time dealing with hiring, management, and human resources issues, so I have started taking actions in my Daily Schedule to remove these items from my life.

CURTIS ESTES'S TO NOT DO LIST (condensed version)

- Detail work like filing, sweeping the kitchen floor, and laundry
- Reading the tax code
- Home fix-it projects
- Exercising on the Stairmaster
- Hiring and management

My own To Not Do List provides me with incentive to create activities in my schedule that move me away from my To Not Do List and closer to my To Be List™. When planning my Daily Schedule, I reflect on those things on my To Not Do List and schedule in activities that help me remove those. When I decided not to sit on the board of an organization, a good use of my time that was robbing me of valuable time I could have been spending with my children, I scheduled in activities such as: "Call Joe to see if he will replace me on the board," and "discuss resignation with president." As reflected in my Daily Schedule[3] from July 1, 2010 on the following page, this list reminds me not only to add activities that move me toward my vision, but also to eliminate, delegate, or reduce those things that do not support my vision.

---

3. To track your Daily Schedule, you can use the day planner or software program you have been using to keep track of your daily appointments.

Curtis's Daily Schedule for July 1, 2010

6 a.m.   Awake and do 50 pushups instead of hitting snooze.

6:15 a.m.   Drive to the club to complete the rest of my exercise regimen for 186 consecutive days of exercise.

8 a.m.   Breakfast meeting with Blake Davenport (egg white omelet, no bacon).

9:30 a.m.   Staff meeting to focus on scheduling more meetings in our office and delegating management duties.

10 a.m.   Estate planning meeting with tax attorney Bob Kopple and prospective client.

11 a.m.   Annual review meeting with Steve Reasner.

12 p.m.   Lunch meeting with Phil Tirone. Order a salad.

1:30 p.m.   Client meeting with Bryce Eddy.

3 p.m.   Team $1 Million networking meeting with Anthony Marguleas and Dave Fenton.

5 p.m.   Work on new puzzles and play with kids after driving home.

6:30 p.m.   Healthy dinner as a family.

7:30 p.m.   Nightly reading, prayers, and bedtime for kids.

8 p.m.   Coordinate upcoming travel schedule with my wife, finish reading *The Freedom Ratio*, skip any sweets.

10 p.m.   Journal my positive focus / best memory for the day. Pray with my wife on our knees before going to sleep.

Spend time creating your To Not Do List in the space provided below, reflecting on your Current Schedule to determine which activities are *shoulds* and thus could be eliminated, delegated, or reduced to a minimum. Reflect also on the Pyramid Flip™ to find those activities in the safe house and outhouse that can be removed from your schedule.

TO NOT DO LIST

Your Life by Design™ is intended to work into your busy schedule, providing transformational exercises that can be completed in just a few short hours. However, because life twists, turns, and changes, the process is ongoing. As such, you must commit to creating a Daily Schedule each day that continues to move you in the direction of your dreams. (Remember also that your Ideal Schedule will change as your life and accomplishments change.) To accommodate the dynamic nature of life, schedule five minutes each day to design your next day's schedule, remembering to consistently work toward your Ideal Schedule. Eventually, this will become habit, the most important part of your day, and will be an ongoing process that points you toward your ideal life.

COACHING TIP:

Another support mechanism to remove activities from your calendar is to change your environment. At Dan Sullivan's suggestion I've given up my office, where I seemed to accumulate stuff and messes, and hired a driver so that I can handle all calls and emails during reclaimed drive time and be fully present once I'm home for the day.

THE FIVE TACTICS FOR IMPLEMENTING YOUR STRATEGIC PLAN

BIGGER VISION

SPECIFIC STRATEGY DRIVEN BY THE COMPELLING WHY

EXACTING IMPLEMENTATION

TRANSFORMING RESULTS

THE FIVE TACTICS FOR IMPLEMENTING YOUR STRATEGIC PLAN

Ability is what you're capable of doing. Motivation determines what you do. Attitude determines how well you do it.
—Lou Holtz

IT HAS BEEN SAID THAT ORDER IS THE FIRST LAW OF HEAVEN. Chaos begets chaos. Calm begets calm. Now that we have rolled up our sleeves and needled our way into every light and dark, fresh and musty, corner and crevice of our lives, we are ready to implement our vision. We have established a principled, targeted, and aligned strategy for wellness and fulfillment. Even with all of these elements in place, all the planning and soul-searching will be for naught without the ability to successfully implement the plan into our lives. In this section, we create the physical and emotional environment that allows you to implement the strategy you created in Section 2.

W. Clement Stone said it best: "So many fail because they don't get started—they don't go. They don't overcome inertia. They don't begin." Have you ever known someone with great potential, a brilliant mind, and a strong personality, but no motivation? Compare this person to someone with a mediocre mind, an ordinary personality, but much motivation. If you had to place your money on someone, who would it be? I would choose motivation over potential any day of the week.

The difference between the person who leads a mediocre, bare, and meaningless life and the person who becomes an all-around superstar is nothing more than determination. The greater a person's determination and perseverance, the greater her success.

Throughout this book, I have called you an overachiever, referring to the success you have achieved in the world's eyes. Now you will truly become a superstar in your own eyes by making the decision to implement the strategy and move from professional success to all-around significance. In this section, you decide who you will be: Here, you truly define whether you are living a life of significance. Here, you will go for the gold, intentionally creating a physical, mental, and emotional environment that supports your goals using five tactics:

- Implementation Tactic #1: Leverage Your Physical, Mental, and Emotional Environment Using the Inspiration Zone™

- Implementation Tactic #2: The Personal Board of Advisors™

- Implementation Tactic #3: The Make Every Day Winnable Game Plan™

- Implementation Tactic #4: Staying Confident by Maintaining the Goals Accomplished Progress Report™

- Implementation Tactic #5: The Family Tree Legacy™

You have designed your life. Now it is time to start living by design.

IMPLEMENTATION TACTIC #1

—Leverage Your Physical, Mental, and Emotional Environment with the Inspiration Zone™

A memorable home celebrates past achievements while inspiring future ones.

—SOTHEBY'S ADVERTISEMENT

NO MATTER WHAT TYPE OF GOALS YOU HAVE SET IN YOUR LIFE, the physical environment in which they breathe is crucial to their growth. Take some time to revamp your home and office environment to allow inspiration, creation, and movement to freely flow by creating an Inspiration Zone™.

If you are not ready to give up your office, start by creating a workspace that is comfortable and compelling. Awaken your senses in every way you possibly can. Post pictures that lift your energy, resonate with your hopes, and ignite those sparks of passion. Hang photos of your family, your children on vacation, a beach house you dream to own, a piece of art work or majestic landscape that takes your breath away. We all have visited inspirational places. Keep physical evidence of these memories close to you. Do not rely on your memory or heartfelt appreciation of these things, trusting that the thought of such inspiration will provoke the same response. Intentionally put objects, pictures, and reminders in places that will provide you that spark when you least expect it but most need it. For example, we took our son to Paris to celebrate his first birthday. Some might think that traveling with a toddler sounds trying, but the vacation was spectacular and filled us with cherished memories. I keep a small Eiffel Tower statue next to my phone as a frequent reminder to keep my focus on making memories instead of having work be solely about money.

COACHING TIP:

Become your personal advertising agency. Why do companies spend millions of dollars on billboards to get us to do what they want? Because it works! Buy a large corkboard for each member of your family or business team. Spend an afternoon attaching affirming pictures and quotes to your corkboard, expressing what they represent to each team or family member. If you dream of a certain home, for instance, find a picture of your dream home and affix it to your "dream board."

As well, be sure to mitigate the forces that tend to distract you. If you find that you are constantly drawn toward checking and responding to emails throughout your workday, then restrict the amount of time you spend on email. Instead of checking every time a new email pops into your inbox, mute the alarm that alerts you to incoming emails and schedule three times per day that you focus your energy on emailing. This way you stand at the helm of leading your ship, and you are able to consciously keep it on course.

Environmental distractions abound in every home and work office. It is your job to create the necessary boundaries and systems that will support goals rather than cause greater diversions. Whenever it is possible, resist the urge to multi-task. Studies prove multi-tasking to be an enormous waste of time that cuts productivity by up to 53 percent.[1] As it is, on average, only three minutes out of every hour are used with maximum focus.

The superstar will create an environment that supports maximum focus, taking ownership of his own attention, behavior, and energy by removing distractions and supplying motivators.

---

1. *NeuroImage* (Aug. 1, 2001).

It has been said that if you change your thinking, you will change your life. The same is true when considering your energy: Elevate your energy and you will elevate your life. Living *Your Life by Design™* requires that you take as much responsibility as possible for turning your internal and external space into an Inspiration Zone™.

Go to WWW.CURTISESTES.BIZ for templates to help you create your **Physical Environment Inspiration Zone™**.

Perhaps even more important than designing an appropriate physical environment is your ability to create a supportive, revitalizing, and inspiring mental and emotional environment. Just as your body can become tired, so can your mind. Reminding it and feeding it is key to your success. Creating and maintaining a piqued state of energy as well as a positive mindset will catapult you closer to your goals. Each of us is responsible for plugging into our own source of energy. We must understand what factors serve as our most effective motivators and sources of energy. Imagine flicking on the light switch without having the lamp plugged into the wall. Nothing would happen. Everything needs energy, including your goals. The trick is to find your own personal outlet to electricity.

Energy boosters can be anything and everything—people, dreams, thoughts, prose, activities, and the like. Perhaps taking a brisk walk refreshes you. Perhaps you like re-reading a favorite poem or calling a good friend. The point is: Find as many sources as you can, plug them into your Daily Schedule, and seek new ones when necessary. No matter what level of success you have achieved, and no matter what walls you have already scaled, without energy boosters in place, you will likely run out of steam and slow down the attainment of your goals.

Robert Cooper, author of *Get Out of Your Own Way*, calls these boosts of energy "auto drivers" and believes them to be an integral component to movement. Auto drivers are simply automatic and consistent triggers that are scattered throughout the day, serving to drive you in the direction you wish to travel. For Cooper these auto drivers range from starting every morning with push-ups, drinking tea, and watching the sunrise while envisioning goals, to speaking to his wife at least two times a day during business travel to further anchor him to his family goals.

Daily exercise is one of the most effective and powerful energy boosters we have available to us and is an essential component in the pursuit of living *Your Life by Design™*. A vibrant and nourished mind and body are required if we are to sustain levels of energy, momentum, and passion in our lives. Tony Robbins insists on an hour of exercise every day, and calls this "an hour of power." (As I mentioned before, I love having a DVD and DVR connected to the television in front of my elliptical trainer so that I can catch up on movies or favorite television shows while exercising.)

Naturally, you will be faced with times when you refuse to take action or when procrastination prevails. Energy boosters will get you moving in the right direction when all else fails. Write them down, keep them close, and use them when necessary. Remember that positive behavior drives positive attitude. If you do not feel like doing something, taking one small and positive step can shift your attitude in a more positive direction.

That said, I urge you to not wait until your motivation is lacking to finally break out your energy arsenal. These boosters must be strategically positioned throughout the course of the day so that, insomuch as is possible, you combat any energy drains before they occur. Do not be a thermometer that only reflects the environment it is in, be the thermostat that sets the environment and makes things happen.

When I am feeling stuck, I try breathing deeply, looking at pictures of fun memories with my family or brochures for my next vacation, and of course, reading Far Side jokes. Energy boosters can be a critical part of driving your ideal day.

An energy-boosting breakthrough that I integrated in January 2010 is the practice of consistent daily exercise. Because I became flaky in my workouts, I committed to exercising in some fashion (even just 100 pushups or stomach crunches) every single day for a week, then for a month. I have now worked out in some fashion for more than 1,000 days, missing only two days when I totally spaced. This has created a "metabolic momentum" that has changed not just my daily energy level, but also my self-image and even the way I vacation. For my last business trip, the first thing I packed was my workout clothes, and after landing in Toronto, I headed straight to the streets for an invigorating run through the city.

Critical also to your emotional environment is the company you keep. When you have finally built the fortress that protects and nurtures your dreams and goals, be cautious of whom you allow to cross the threshold. Those people who are granted access to your home and life will certainly alter the environment for better or worse. Surround yourself with positive, uplifting people that sustain and fuel your energy level. These people are easy to recognize, as you feel alive and energized in their presence. The same philosophy applies to those who drain and exhaust you. Identify the culprits. Avoid these "energy vampires" like the plague. If need be, buy a silver cross to keep the danger away. The burden of life is heavy enough without inviting "black holes" into your personal space. Remove those people that are not aligned with your passions and intentions. Do so with grace but without regret. No precaution is too great when fulfillment of your ideal life is at stake.

For those closest friends, whose very presence nourishes you, consider a standing weekly call. I have breakfast with Brett every Tuesday and 5:30 am calls with Ethan on Wednesdays and Phil on Saturdays. They are scheduled for an hour but we have no agenda. Matthew Kelley writes in *Rhythm of Life* that the best way to go deeper is by wasting time together, not that the hour is wasted but only that we give ourselves space to share whatever is on our minds from our deepest concerns to the recent hilarious comedy.

Go to **www.curtisestes.biz** for templates to help you create your **Mental and Emotional Inspiration Zone**.™

Viktor Frankel wrote, "You do not simply exist, but always decide what your life will be, and what you will become in the next moment."[2] Once you begin to act on what matters to you, even by making the smallest change in your perspective or behavior, psychological daylight appears. All kinds of change-oriented adjustments take place in your makeup. You shift from potential energy to kinetic energy. Your senses open up. Your neurochemistry becomes more primed to change a bit more, and then a bit more after that,[3] assisting you in leading *Your Life by Design*™.

---

2. V. Frankel, *Man's Ultimate Search for Meaning* (New York: Perseus, 2000).
3. J. Loehr, *Stress for Success* (*TimesBusiness,* 1999); J. Loehr and T. Schwartz, *The Power of Full Engagement* (New York: *Free Press,* 2003); R.A. Dienstbier, in L. Miller, "To Beat Stress, Get Tough," *Psychology Today* (Nov. 1989).

Energy Boosters

Grab a pen and list your energy boosters in the space below, and post the list on the wall of your office, and on your refrigerator at home.

IMPLEMENTATION TACTIC #2

—The Personal Board of Advisors™

*Keep away from people who try to belittle your ambitions. Small
people always do that, but the really great people make you feel that
you, too, can become great.*
—MARK TWAIN

CRITICAL TO CREATING AN INSPIRING EMOTIONAL ENVIRONMENT is the
support of a network that applauds your success and cheers you on, holding
you accountable, brainstorming for solutions, and helping you along the way.
Having coworkers and employees who believe in you and support the "new you"
is a major component of staying in the zone. Hopefully, you have a supportive
network of family and friends. Regardless, I suggest creating a Personal Board
of Advisors™ which functions similar to the way a business's board of directors
does. The purpose of your Personal Board of Advisors™ is to create a group of
like-minded and inspiring superstars who will exchange ideas and construc-
tively critique your strategies.

Your first step is to identify approximately eight individuals with an interest
in you and your personal and professional success, people who have taken a
sincere interest in your development and who have accomplished a lot in their
own right. My Personal Board of Advisors™ is filled with people I would like

to emulate, including my best clients, best friends, and other well accomplished (and well integrated) people. Your Personal Board of Advisors™ will convene annually to exchange ideas and assess your progress, lending you fresh perspective about your goals, strategies, vision, and balance.

Once you have identified these individuals, send a letter similar to the one included below, which you can also download from **WWW.CURTISESTES.BIZ**.

Personal Board of Advisors™ Letter

Dear _____:

I hope this note finds you in good spirits. The purpose of this letter is to let you know of my continued commitment to leading a life by design. That is, I am committed to leading a significant life whereby I pursue both my personal and professional aspirations. Because I have such deep admiration for your remarkable success, I would like to draw upon your experience, good sense, and wisdom as I strategize to reach my own goals.

I am bringing together a board of advisors that includes successful individuals from diverse fields of life to exchange ideas and critique my strategies. Your participation would include an annual dinner meeting of the board of advisors. At this meeting, I will outline my vision and introduce my strategies for the coming year. In addition, I will share how I would like you to keep me accountable so that I am sure to meet my goals.

Our kick-off meeting is scheduled for _____ at _____ p.m. at _____ in _____. Attached, please find a list of the others invited. I think you will find them a stimulating group and the gathering rewarding in and of itself.

Please expect my call early next week to see if you will be able to join me as an even more meaningful partner in my growth. Thank you for your consideration.

With warm regards,

_____

Remember that when your Personal Board of Advisors™ meets, you are the chairman and will be responsible for the agenda. During the meetings, be sure that your agenda includes:

- **Introductions of the members of your Personal Board of Advisors™.** Allow your board to spend a few minutes each talking about themselves, their personal interests, and why they chose to join your board.

- **Reminder of the purpose and goals of the Personal Board of Advisors™.** Let the board members know that you are joining together to exchange ideas. Assure them that you welcome constructive criticism, and that you want honest assessment of your strategies. Let them know, as well, that their main job is to hold you accountable. If you promise to do something by the next meeting, you want them to hold you accountable to your word.

- **Introduction to your vision.** Spend several minutes telling your board about your overall vision, as well as where you stand in relation to that vision.

- **An outline of your goals for the next quarter.** Explain how you will spend the next quarter moving closer and closer to your vision. What are the SMART goals you will accomplish between now and your next meeting?

- **Input and commitment from your board about these goals.** If you have chosen a strong Personal Board of Advisors™, your board members will likely have their own ideas about your strategies. As well, if they know you personally, they might know of any obstacles you face or shortcomings you must overcome to meet your goals. Encourage honest but productive feedback.

- **Your promise of accountability (see Strategy Component #4: The Rewards and Consequences Multiplier™).** Conclude the meeting by promising your board members that you will move forward on the action steps to which you have committed. Remind the board of its purpose and promise them that you will not waste their time by failing to make use of their suggestions.

For a sample Personal Board of Advisors™ agenda, see WWW.CURTISESTES. BIZ. After the meeting, do not forget to send monthly email status reports and take one or two board members to lunch quarterly to discuss fine-tuning your plan and whether you have been accountable.

Regular meetings with your Personal Board of Advisors™ are critical to address the constant changes in your life. As life changes, so too will your goals. Currently, I am focusing on financial goals that I know will change. At this time, I am working to put a financial cap on my material standard of living, and then over time, I want to maintain this cap, even while I earn more, so that I can give more. During the course of my life, I want to donate $100 million to charity. While I still have a long way to go before reaching the goal, the vision gives me tremendous energy.

With this in mind, I am aware that I must regularly update my life plan so that it continues to be a life of my design. If I allow myself to lapse into complacency, I will soon fall into a life by default. *Your Life by Design™* is not a one-time planning session; it requires constant maintenance, a shifting of strategies, and a refocusing of energies. By creating a Personal Board of Advisors™, you will have an automatic system for continuing to evaluate your strategy and move the design of your life forward.

IMPLEMENTATION TACTIC #3

—The Make Every Day Winnable Game Plan™

> *You can't do anything about yesterday. The door to the past has been shut and the key thrown away. You can do nothing about tomorrow. It is yet to come. However, tomorrow is in large part determined by what you do today. So make today a masterpiece. You have control over that.*
>
> —JOHN WOODEN

A SUCCESSFUL LIFE IS NOTHING MORE THAN A SUCCESSION of successful days. But what makes for a successful day?

Whenever we contemplate changing our lives in significant ways it is easy to become overwhelmed, thinking that we have to accomplish everything to feel as though we have accomplished anything. But the fact is that the day is seldom as long as our "to do" lists.

The solution is not to throw up our hands in exasperation or bow our heads in resignation. The solution is to make every day winnable by identifying the three things that, if we do each and

> **COACHING TIP:**
> *Adopt Robert Pagliarini's tip. Before you turn your doorknob to walk into your home, stop. Pause to release any pent-up tension. Consider how you will connect with your family. Then enter. This will help you clear your head and be fully present.*

COACHING TIP:

When you *set a goal, you create momentum. However, that momentum diminishes radically if you do not do anything about it after three days; after 12 days, the momentum is all but gone. Set small, winnable goals now, and take action immediately.*

every day, will pay the greatest dividends.

In my case, if I do 50 pushups, keep five meetings with great clients, and spend at least one hour of uninterrupted time "being present" (playing, reading, or rolling around on the floor) with my children, my day has been a victory. The important thing is to make sure that the achievement of these goals is under your control, specifically defined and measurable, and realizable every day.

For the past five years, I've taken the strategy to the next level by writing down my three specific biggest wins for the day in a journal and also reviewing my next day's schedule and writing down and VISUALIZING the three biggest wins I want to have tomorrow. It's seemingly divine intervention considering how often I achieve the wins I visualize.

Remember, big changes do not happen over night. They are the result of small improvements made each and every day.

The Make Every Day Winnable Game Plan™

Write your three Make Every Day Winnable Game Plan™ goals in the space provided below:

1. _____

2. _____

3. _____

Evaluate the progress you make regularly and update your Make Every Day Winnable Game Plan™ goals as needed to keep you engaged and growing.

IMPLEMENTATION TACTIC #4

—Staying Confident by Maintaining the Goals Accomplished Progress Report™

Honor every rung on the ladder of life.
—Jeff Photiades

AS YOU BEGIN LIVING THE LIFE YOU HAVE DESIGNED, it is essential not just to track your progress, but also to do so in a way that motivates you to continue growing and improving.

If a person measures success by looking at the distances he has yet to travel, he will always be disappointed. If, on the other hand, he measures success by the distance he has already traveled, he will see that he has already reached great success.

Consider the young man who walks into an important meeting. He is riddled with insecurity because he believes himself to not be as accomplished as the businessmen and women he is about to meet. His suit is not expensive enough, his résumé not impressive enough, his car not new enough. This man is measuring his worthiness by the distance he must travel to reach his goals.

Consider, on the other hand, a similar man. He wears the same off-the-rack suit, has limited experience, and drives a battered car. Yet this man walks into the same meeting with his head held high, shoulders back, and proud to be a self-taught man who overcame great obstacles to walk into a business meeting with such accomplished men and women. He cares not about the distance ahead of him, but rather about the distance he has already traveled from his starting point.

COACHING TIP:

Consider starting a journal that documents your best memories for the day. I have been doing this for 1,945 days. Jordan, my oldest son, regularly asks me to read to him from my "Best Memories" book. This reminds us of all the precious time we have spent together, and it inspires us to create more best memories. After particularly fun events, Jordan says, "I'll bet this will be today's best memory!"

Both men have the same abilities, education, and level of accomplishment. Only their perspectives are different. What perspective better serves the seeker? *Your Life by Design™* promotes the latter perspective, encouraging overachievers to document and celebrate milestones of progress in relation to their starting point.

The best way to track your progress so as to continually increase your motivation is to create a Goals Accomplished Progress Report™. Your Goals Accomplished Progress Report™ will be a living document that lists all of the goals you have accomplished and the things for which you are thankful.

You should update your Goals Accomplished Progress Report™ regularly, at least every few weeks, allowing it to become your autobiography. I have kept a Goals Accomplished Progress Report™ for a decade, and it is tremendously rewarding to look back at how far I have come and how much fun I have had. Likewise, you will notice from my own report below, that the Goals Accomplished Progress Report™ consists not just of the big victories, but also of the simple joys that bring a smile to my face. Here is my 2009-10 report as an example.

Curtis Estes's 2009-2010 Goals Accomplished Progress Report™ (condensed version)

1. An extraordinary evening of dancing with Kristi at Kerrigan's Black Tie Dinner after spending the day with Jordan at the Northern Trust Open.
2. First father-daughter dance with Vyvien at Bel Air Presbyterian Church, a terrific evening.
3. Both Blake and Ron identified my brand as being a "strategic breakthrough partner" on the same day.
4. First opportunity to serve communion as an elder—very humbling.
5. Jordan asked me to read to him from the best memories journal.
6. Inspired by Keith Phillips's huge service for the Kingdom through World Impact.
7. Christian Curtis Estes is born! Amazing to have three children. We are going to have so much fun together as a family.
8. I take Jordan and Vyvien to Bel Air Country Club for the afternoon where we chip, putt, rake the sand and feed the ducks.
9. Ann, Linda, Beth and I start the Network of Executive Women to Harness the Power of Influential Women in Business in LA
10. Jordan, Vyvien and I take "the longest walk ever" from the Jonathan Beach Club to the pier and back, racing along the surf.
11. Terrific time at the Rosewood Mayakoba with Team Kerrigan enjoying beach runs daily, getting the first cabana, and Skyping with my family.
12. Great first date with mom and more to come.
13. Jordan, Vyvien, and I start, and ultimately finish, Van Gogh's "The Bedroom" 1,000-piece puzzle.
14. Creating thankfulness ornaments with the family after Thanksgiving to be hung on the Christmas tree.
15. Jordan and Vyvien ride their bikes with training wheels for the first time ever and do a great job.
16. Launch the Parents Education League with Desiree to provide families a one-stop resource to navigate the private school admissions process in LA.
17. Jordan is very sad and concerned to learn that some people he loves don't know Jesus because he wants to be with them forever in Heaven.
18. Jordan, Vyvien, and Daddy create Christmas decorations with Bel Air Presbyterian Church for the Hope Gardens families.
19. Jordan and Vyvien are both in the Christmas Concert with a speaking part for Jordan as a shepherd and Vyvien as an angel.

20. Great afternoon with the kids taking a long bike ride throughout the neighborhood and playing with the remote control car and helicopter.
21. Christian has his first formal dining experience at The Loft at Montage, while Kristi and I enjoyed delicious short-rib stew and cheese course, accompanied by a 1999 Silver Oak.
22. Celebrate Kristi's birthday with breakfast in bed served by Jordan, Vyvien, mom and myself, followed by an afternoon, "big, big dance party" in the den.
23. Have terrific lunch with Kristi and Bob Kerrigan about how Kristi can become more who she is.
24. Bring together Nolan Bushnell, Rob Flutie, Flint Dilly, and Andrew Breitbart to elect the next U.S. Senator, revolutionize education, and bust the unions.
25. Have a sock-monkey sleep-over party with Jordan, Vyvien, Kristi, and Grandma.
26. Enjoy the mayor's prayer breakfast with Bishop Kenneth Ulmer rocking the house, followed by playing Crazy Eights with Jordan and Vyvien in the afternoon.
27. 200 hundred guests join us at the $30 million house with $10 million of cars in the 20-car motor court for our NEXUS-LA Lamborghini event.
28. Heart-warming smiles from Christian and hugs and kisses from Vyvien, after which I promised she could get anything she wanted with a big hug and a kiss.
29. Successful first speech to Matt Russo and Jim Nemec's offices in New York City, raising over $50,000 for Bel Air Preschool, followed by lunch with Matt at the Grand Central Oyster Bar.
30. Bring our neighbors, the Palumbos, to Bel Air Presbyterian and enjoy a family afternoon at David Houck's with little C and little D.
31. Best Mornings with Dad fire station field trip with Jordan and Vyvien. They love "driving" the fire trucks.
32. Have a meeting with Mike and two gentlemen to help bring the NFL back to Los Angeles.
33. Teach Jordan how to win at tic-tac-toe, then teach Jordan and Vyvien how to play chess, which Jordan picks up even faster than tic-tac-toe.
34. I am blessed to serve in the foot-washing station for the Maundy Thursday service, washing feet of both my mom and Ruth Jervis.
35. Jordan, Vyvien, and Christian, Kristi, and I celebrate a glorious Easter at the Hollywood Bowl with Bel Air Presbyterian Church.

36. Thanks to Blake, begin reading Charles Spurgeon's *Morning and Evening* daily devotional.
37. Jordan, Vyvien, and Daddy do a Jonathan Club beach trip to catch sand crabs using our new fish nets, where Vyvien also creates several excellent sand angels.
38. Partner with Christian Magoon and Margaret to use the Financial Security Score to help create the most financially secure communities in America.
39. Jordan and Vyvien create their first art installation at the Estes residence.
40. We learn that Jordan is accepted to the Curtis School kindergarten, while I am honored to be at Whitworth University electing Beck Taylor as their 18th president.
41. Vyvien tells me, "I want you to sleep with me forever and I won't change my mind."
42. With Kristi's signature, commit to Canyon Ranch Life Enhancement Program funded by Strategic Coach referral bonus.
43. When I asked her what she learned that day at Bible Study Fellowship, Vyvien shares that she learned that Jesus died to wash away our sins so that we could be together in Heaven forever.

This Goals Accomplished Progress Report™ keeps me focused on all the great things happening in my life. It is a reminder of the positive momentum I have. By keeping an updated list in my *Life by Design Manual*™, I stay motivated during difficult times. Now it is your turn. In the space provided, list your achievements over the past year and the things for which you are thankful.

Goals Accomplished Progress Report™

IMPLEMENTATION TACTIC #5

—The Family Tree Legacy™

Every day you have a chance to be a transforming presence in the lives of those around you.
—EDITH VARLEY

YEARS AGO, WHILE ATTENDING A SEMINAR, the speaker of the event selected me from the crowd and asked me to share the names of my great-grandparents. I could not name one of them. I was mortified. While my initial reaction was sheer embarrassment, before long it became frustration and concern that my great-grandchildren might not know my name. The thought that my great-grandchildren might not know my name deeply affected me. It seemed impossible considering how much grandparents dote on their grandkids, the intense love, commitment, and obligation they feel for them and the effectual contribution they make to their lives. How could a grandchild's child not know the names of these loving, affectionate family members who played such an important role?

In asking this question to colleagues and clients, I have learned that I am not alone in being unable to recollect the names of relatives I think I should know. The reality is that unless you do something really good or really bad, your family will forget you in three generations, or about 88 years. In less than a century, the odds are that your great-grandchildren will not know your name, much less what you stood for or what your hopes and dreams were for them.

You might say, "Wait a minute! My future generations will inherit my wealth and they will remember me for that!" But passing on only money to future generations is not enough. It is much more important to plan, document, and share personal values and goals as a way to give your great-grandchildren something to remember you by. Too many people think of a legacy as an inheritance—something they leave behind after they die. But as a student of *Your Life by Design™*, you know better. Once you have designed your own life, it is time to design a legacy while you are still alive, a legacy that can continue once you are gone. Sharing your values as well as your wealth will ensure that your branch on the family tree is a living limb, not just dead wood. To assure your legacy lasts more than a generation, I suggest incorporating a Family Tree Legacy™ into your strategic plan.

My inability to recall the names of my great-grandparents coupled with the birth of my first child prompted me to create the Estes Family Tree Legacy, a 188-year plan for transferring the values I want to pass on to future Estes generations. The plan incorporates:

- The values I want to pass along to our children, grandchildren and great-grandchildren.

- The primary tools to pass these values on; and

- A chronological listing of milestones I want to celebrate in the 100-plus years I plan to live. (As a healthy, active male living in the twenty-first century, I truly believe our generation can and will live well beyond the age of 100, thanks to modern medicine, health care, exercise, and nutrition.)

Now is the time to begin working on your Family Tree Legacy™, even if your children are grown. Start with these simple steps:

1. Identify the values you want to pass on to your family, such as faith, education, charity, entrepreneurship, goal setting, or community involvement.

2. Establish incentives that will integrate your values in the family for future generations. For example, if you value education, set up a trust fund that will pay for your future generations' tuition.

3. Create tools and fund these incentives to ensure that they last over time. If you want your great-grandchildren to attend your alma mater, support your college through endowments and scholarships to help maintain its academic strength and viability for years to come.

The following is my Family Tree Legacy™.

Estes Family Tree Legacy™

Values I want to pass on to future Estes generations:

- Christian faith and evangelism
- Love of family
- Educational excellence
- Charity
- Entrepreneurship
- Goal setting and personal growth
- Community service
- Carpe Diem—Having fun while seizing the day

Incentives to encourage future generations to appreciate the above values:

- Education funded 100 percent for pre-school through bachelor of science degree.

- $10,000 a year (increased with inflation) personal improvement grant for a Strategic Coach®-type program.

- Access to a matched earning fund up to $100,000 a year. If they are a teacher or in the ministry, they will receive $2 for every $1 that they earn, or if they are an entrepreneur they will receive $1 for every $2 that they earn.

- $1,000 a day for up to 10 days per year spent doing charitable work, encouraging them to donate the money back to the organization.

- $1 million Northwestern Mutual life insurance policy funded for them from birth through college.

- Upon their graduation from college, on their birthday every year, I will fund a long weekend at the Four Seasons or equivalent resort.

Primary tools to pass on these values:

- Set aside $5 million for our family's education using a dynasty trust.

- Set aside $5 million for the capitalism-matching fund for future generations.

- Establish $100,000 written goal reward/encouragement fund.

- Set aside $10 million for the Estes Family Foundation making five percent annual grants with children's involvement in selecting the charities and, ideally, participation with the recipient organizations.

- Give $1 million to the National Center for Fathering and the International Justice Mission.

- Give $10 million to Bel Air Presbyterian Church to fund the elementary school.

- Give $10 million to Bel Air Presbyterian Church's endowment for missionaries.

- Give $10 million to Pacifica Christian High School to endow Honors Scholarships.

- Give $5 million to Whitworth University for the Polhemus Hall for Inspired Leaders.

- Give $25 million to Whitworth University for a scholarship endowment.

- Consider donating success and religion sections to libraries, fund high school classes for financial planning and a goal setting curriculum, and hire a family values "historian."

- Consider "financially" adopting some kids, perhaps for my relative's children, a friend's child, or a needy child from Bel Air Presbyterian Church.

Chronological milestones:

- 2015: Grow Bigger Futures Press to a 100-author publishing house raising $500,000+ annually for transformational charities.
- 2016: Be the first trustee in residence at Whitworth University.
- 2017: Jordan joins the inaugural seventh-grade class at Pacifica Christian High School.
- 2018: I turn 50 years old and celebrate by buying a residence on the Utopia cruise ship and spend summers abroad raising the kids as global citizens while hosting missionaries ready for rest and rejuvenation.
- 2019: Family mission trip to Asia with the International Justice Mission.
- 2020: Renew our vows at Greystone mansion celebrating my 20th wedding anniversary with Kristi.
- 2021: 30 years affiliation with Northwestern Mutual, spend the entire year abroad with my family.
- 2022: Jordan begins college, perhaps Whitworth University.
- 2023: Join Jordan during summer internship at Northwestern Mutual's headquarters.
- 2024: Vyvien begins college.
- 2025: Move to a home on Bel Air Country Club's golf course after reaching the goal of giving away $50 million.
- 2026: Begin our family foundation engaging our children in philanthropy.
- 2027: Spend a weekend at the White House, and Christian begins college.
- 2028: I turn 60 years old and celebrate with friends in Italy.
- 2029: Orbit the Earth with Virgin Galactic.
- 2030: Celebrate my 30th wedding anniversary with Kristi at the Grand-Hotel du Cap-Ferrat.
- 2031: 40 years affiliation with Northwestern Mutual.
- 2032: Fund the Estes family education dynasty trust.
- 2033: Endow Pacifica Christian High School Honors Scholarships.
- 2034: Help Whitworth University raise its endowment to $1 billion.

- 2035: Have given away $100 million; endow capitalism-matching fund.
- 2036: Start programs for five other universities to get to $1 billion endowments.
- 2037: Fund Bel Air Presbyterian Church missionary endowment.
- 2038: I turn 70 years old and celebrate with friends in Australia.
- 2039: Our children start blessing us with grandchildren.
- 2040: Celebrate my 40th wedding anniversary with Kristi at the Post Ranch Inn.
- 2041: 50 years affiliation with Northwestern Mutual.
- 2042: Fund Whitworth University scholarship endowment.
- 2043: Open the Creation Museum showcasing art that celebrates Creation.
- 2044: Fund the Success and Christian literature sections of one library per year going forward.
- 2048: Shoot my age, 80, at Bel Air Country Club.

And so on through 2100: with my legacy being built upon by future Estes generations.

Using my family legacy as an example, you can see how I have linked values to intentional activities that benefit my family for many generations. I value education, so I plan to set aside money for a family education dynasty trust. Rather than simply inherit money, I want the Estes children to work for their inheritance. As an example, the entrepreneurs in the family will receive $1 for every $2 they earn. And because I value social service, I will give $2 for every $1 earned by those who become teachers, missionaries, or ministers. I would also like to remind my children, grandchildren, and their descendents to have fun, so on their birthdays every year after graduating college, I will fund a long weekend at a Four Seasons or equivalent resort of their choice. (Surely, this will help them remember my name.)

In his book, Bret Baier writes, "Totally above and beyond any career achievements in television or journalism, if one day I was able to look up and see my son living his life to the fullest with joy and gratefulness in his heart and a spirit of helping others around him, I would count my own life a success."

I echo Bret's sentiments and hope to follow his example in raising kids that put service before self and lead a life of much greater joy in the process.

A family legacy plan does not have to be complicated, but you can see why it is first necessary to get clear about your own personal vision, values, and goals. Reflecting back on the vision, values, and goals you formulated during the *Your Life by Design™* process, outline your Family Tree Legacy™ in the space provided below.

Family Tree Legacy™

Values to pass on: _____

_____

_____

_____

_____

_____

_____

_____

_____

_____

_____

_____

_____

Incentives to encourage future generations to appreciate the above values:

_____

_____

_____

_____

_____

_____

_____

_____

Primary tools to pass on these values: _____

_____

_____

_____

_____

_____

_____

_____

_____

Chronological milestones: _____

_____

_____

_____

_____

_____

_____

_____

_____

_____

THE FOUR SECRETS FOR OBTAINING TRANSFORMATIONAL RESULTS

BIGGER VISION

SPECIFIC STRATEGY DRIVEN BY THE COMPELLING WHY

EXACTING IMPLEMENTATION

TRANSFORMING RESULTS

THE FOUR SECRETS FOR OBTAINING TRANSFORMATIONAL RESULTS

I have missed more than 9,000 shots in my career. I have lost almost 300 games. On 26 occasions I have been entrusted to take the game winning shot—and I missed. I have failed over and over and over again in my life. And that is precisely why I succeed.

—MICHAEL JORDAN

THOUGH THE OLYMPIC GAMES WERE THE MOST FAMOUS in all of Ancient Greece, the Panathenaic Festival was the most prestigious set of games in the city of Athens, and among the grandest in the entirety of Greece. Held every four years, the festival included musical contests, athletic contests, and boat races. It culminated in a two-mile torch relay race in which four runners from 10 tribes were to run from Eros to the Acropolis.

The goal of the torch race was not to be the first to finish, but to finish the race without causing the torch to go out. To win this race was considered a great triumph.

In *Your Life by Design*™ you have the same goal as the Panathenaic runners: Finish the race with your torch burning brightly.

As you move forward in creating *Your Life by Design*™, remember that the number one reason people succeed is because they persist. They simply decide that they will not give in. They will not quit. In the words of Gary Hames, managing partner for Northwestern Mutual in Kansas City, "The person who wants to, finds a way."

With this in mind, we have four final secrets for your success.

- Secret to Your Success #1: Complete a *Life by Design Manual*™

- Secret to Your Success #2: Weekly Breakthrough Testing

- Secret to Your Success #3: Enjoy the Journey While Charging Toward *Your Life by Design*™

- Secret to Your Success #4: Dare To Be Bold: Expect Epiphanies

SECRET TO YOUR SUCCESS #1

—Complete Your Life by Design Manual™

Until one is committed, there is hesitancy, the chance to draw back. Concerning all acts of initiative (and creation), there is one elementary truth that ignorance of which kills countless ideas and splendid plans: that the moment one definitely commits oneself, then Providence moves too. All sorts of things occur to help one that would never otherwise have occurred. A whole stream of events issues from the decision, raising in one's favor all manner of unforeseen incidents and meetings and material assistance, which no man could have dreamed would have come his way. Whatever you can do, or dream you can do, begin it. Boldness has genius, power, and magic in it. Begin it now.
—Johann Wolfgang von Goethe

WHEN DESIGNING YOUR LIFE, YOU NEED A TOOL THAT ENCAPSULATES your vision and outlines your strategic plan. All your work in this book comes together in a *Life by Design Manual™*. The practice of writing down the goals you have set for yourself is as important as the goal itself. People often make the assumption that to think about, understand, and define their goals eradicates the need to physically write the goal out—pen to paper. This is a mistake. There is unseen power in the practice of writing your goals. The simple act of writing down goals increases the likelihood of achieving them dramatically. Urban legend tells the story of the 1953 graduating class of Yale, three percent of whom had written specific goals for their future while in college. Two decades later, so the story goes, these three percent were worth more financially than the other 97 percent combined. Okay, so the story is an urban legend, unbeknownst to life coaches and motivational speakers across the world. But it *should* be true, and if the study were ever conducted, it likely would be true. According to one study, people who regularly record specific daily and weekly results and goals are nearly 50 percent more likely to make continued progress as those who do not.

The power of not only setting but also writing goals is significant. By committing your goals to paper, you accomplish a number of things: 1) You set the goal in motion; 2) You take ownership and accountability; 3) You have something tangible to reference and affirm your desired intention; and 4) Unseen forces step forward on your behalf. Writing out goals serves as a sacred contract between you and your ideal self, a declaration for your future.

Rewriting your goals is of equal importance. Goals kept at the forefront of your mind will keep you on alert and focused. Consider re-writing your top three goals every morning upon waking, as well as revisiting your most compelling five-year goals before sleeping. Writing, pondering, and envisioning your goals will program your subconscious and propel you forward. "People who grasp their own original goals in distinctive and specific ways are 50 percent more likely to take confident actions to achieve those goals, and a third more likely to feel a sense of control under stressful conditions," says T. Ferris.[1]

Writing down goals holds you accountable, roots your desires and increases your likelihood of success, while engaging the laws of Heaven and Earth to shift and align on your behalf. Writing these intentional words will offer daily boosts of personal affirmation and excitement.

Creating physical evidence of the work you have accomplished herein is the pinnacle and cumulative effect of the *Your Life by Design*™ process. By creating a manual containing the critical worksheets herein, you have physical blueprints of your design plans. In addition to reminding you of your vision and goals, this manual can include pictures of your dream home, dream car, or dream vacation,

---

1. T. Ferris, *The Mind's Sky: Human Intelligence in a Cosmic Context Matters* (Boston: Houghton Mifflin, 1998).

reminding you and providing a mental jumpstart should you start to lose focus. This is another example of how you can become your own personal advertising agency by promoting the life you have designed, making it more likely to come into existence.

If you would like help creating your manual, refer to the Coaching Options on page 150 or visit **WWW.CURTISESTES.BIZ**, where you can download the forms and worksheets or purchase an official *Life by Design Manual™*. To create your own manual, I recommend using a three ring binder with labeled dividers, containing all your completed *Your Life by Design™* statements, exercises, and worksheets. You may also wish to include a section for notes to capture your evolving vision.

The following is a guideline for how you can organize your *Life by Design Manual™*:

1. Your Creating the Bigger Vision™ statement.

2. The SMART Goals Action Plan™ using the SMART Goals Formula™ listing each goal with its compelling *why*, as well as how you will be held accountable. (Visit **WWW.CURTISESTES.BIZ** for a comprehensive Action Plan and Accountability™ worksheet.) This and your Daily Schedule are the two documents you will update the most often.

3. The Ideal Day™ Worksheet. Remember that you should take steps daily that move your Daily Schedule closer and closer to its ideal state.

4. The Make Every Day Winnable Game Plan™.

5. The Goals Accomplished Progress Report™.

6. Your Highlight Reel™.

7. Your Flipped Pyramid Worksheet: The Ideal™.

8. Your Unique Ability® statement.

9. The To Be List™.

10. Your Personal Legacy™.

11. The Family Tree Legacy™.

For examples of the *Life by Design Manual™*, visit **WWW.CURTISESTES.BIZ**, where you can see my manual, as well as other manuals uploaded by *Your Life by Design™* community members. Remember that it is important to review and refine your workbook every day for the first 30 days. Additionally, choose a close friend with whom you want to share it and commit to reviewing your progress with them every quarter. (By visiting **WWW.CURTISESTES.BIZ**, you can also upload it to share your progress and commitments with other *Your Life by Design™* community members.)

SECRET TO YOUR SUCCESS #2

—Weekly Breakthrough Testing

The future?
I have it in my hands today.
What about you?
—W. Edwards Deming

ACCORDING TO ROBERT COOPER, THE BRAIN DOESN'T EVEN WAKE UP until there is urgency around an emotionally compelling goal. And our brains do not feel this urgency until the deadline is within seven days. I suggest, therefore, that you start measuring your progress in weekly, seven-day timeframes to leverage your brain's natural wiring. Letting your brain know that you will measure the results of your goals will help it awaken and take action.

I have been testing this strategy for 275 weeks. After setting goals, I measure what worked, what I learned, and what I want to do next. For instance, my father passed away last year, and my mom now lives with us. I want to let her know what a tremendous help she is to our family and how much I love her, so I set the goal of looking my mom in the eyes and giving her a big hug every time she or I comes home from work. At the end of the week, I measured my progress, taking account of what worked, what I learned, and what I want to do next.

What worked is that I was able to show appreciation for my mom and for all that she does. That week, my mom fell and fractured her hip, requiring surgery. So, *what I learned* is that you never know when a person you love might not come home because she has to go to the hospital instead. My mom recovered after three weeks of recuperation, but I was reminded of how fragile and precious good health is. *What's next* is that I want to keep loving my mom and letting her know how much she contributes to my life at every opportunity.

Here is another example of measuring my breakthroughs each week. As you might have guessed, I have loads of admiration for Robert Cooper. In fact, he is one of my mentors. He recently asked me if I wanted to become dramatically more interesting.

My immediately response was, "Of course!"

But what would that take? I wondered. It sounds like something you either have or don't have, and I have never considered myself to be particularly interesting.

Becoming more interesting is easier than you think. According to Cooper's research, the key is to simply pay better attention to those with whom you are interacting. In fact, if you begin paying someone just 10 percent more attention, the person will react with a 100 percent increase in the amount of felt trust.

The idea was so compelling to me; I immediately wanted to be dramatically more interesting. But I was still a little stuck with how I would implement this.

Then I remembered an article about Ronald Reagan, arguably among the most charming leaders in our time. President Reagan was known for giving a person the feeling that he or she was the only one in the room. While a guest at the Beverly Hills Hotel, President Reagan was once dining in the Polo Lounge when a waiter asked him the secret to his charm.

President Reagan told the waiter that in an effort to engage a person quickly, he would always look directly into the person's face and silently identify his or her eye color. In that fashion, he was quickly able to show the other person that he was paying exceptional attention.

How often is it that we go through an entire day, meeting many different people, and at the end of the day, not know one person's eye color, much less everyone's name? Yet when someone looks directly into your eyes, don't you always feel special?

Paying exceptional attention is, in fact, critical to having a life by design because we must rely on those around us to help us reach success.

Over the next week, use this as one of your weekly breakthroughs to success so that you too can become dramatically more interesting. With your new vision for your life by design, draw a straight line from where you are to where you are going. To become who you want to be, you will identify numerous small changes necessary to make this metamorphosis. As the second secret to your success, every week pick one of these breakthroughs to test, which will get your brain fully engaged. At the end of the week, ask yourself:

- *What worked?*

- *What did I learn?*

- *What's next?*

Visit **WWW.CURTISESTES.BIZ** to see more than 500 examples of my weekly breakthrough testing. Submit and share your weekly breakthrough test to the community section on the website and I will email you my new breakthrough tests for that week!

SECRET TO YOUR SUCCESS #3

—Enjoy the Journey While Charging Toward *Your Life by Design*™

> *Happiness is neither virtue nor pleasure nor this thing nor that but simply growth. We are happy when we are growing.*
> —WILLIAM BUTLER YEATS

WHILE SETTING GOALS IS CRUCIAL TO SUCCESSFUL LIVING, for the over-achiever the process of setting goals can be a dangerous one. We tend to chase goals, constantly measuring our worthiness by whether we have achieved aggressive goals. We become obsessed, sacrificing our lives to the achievement of goals, failing to recognize that if we do not enjoy the process of pursuing our goals, we will not enjoy our lives. Consider this from Oswald Chambers, a twentieth century Scottish Protestant minister and author of one of my favorite books, *My Utmost for His Highest*:

> *"What we see as only the process of reaching a particular end, God sees as the goal itself...*

> *"It is the process, not the outcome, that is glorifying to God. God's training is for now, not later. His purpose is for this very minute, not for sometime in the future. We have nothing to do with what will follow our obedience, and*

we are wrong to concern ourselves with it. What people call preparation, God sees as the goal itself.

"God's purpose is to enable me to see that He can walk on the storms of my life right now. If we have a further goal in mind, we are not paying enough attention to the present time. However, if we realize that moment-by-moment obedience is the goal, then each moment as it comes is precious."

Those well schooled in transformational work, religious or otherwise, recognize this concept as "living in the present." This concept embraces the idea that goals are a tool, not the reason, for existence. Though achievement of the goal is considered a bonus, pursuit of the goal—and the enjoyment that comes out of this—is the ideal. While the most common approach used to measure success is a person's accomplishments, this is hardly the most effective way to measure success, and it fails to serve your ultimate happiness. It is an overachiever's inclination to constantly push limits, so by the time he reaches a goal, he has likely set a new goal that is bigger and more demanding. In this way, goals are like a horizon, constantly moving and often unreachable. For the young overachiever, the goal might be a salary of $100,000 a year. However, by the time he reaches this salary, he has already set the bar higher to $200,000, then $1 million, and so on and so forth. Ultimately, most goals are never reached because by the time the seeker has arrived at the destination determined by the goal, the goal has shifted, stretched, or changed entirely. But this is good news: Setting goals, constantly pushing oneself, and moving toward a greater idea is how one builds a prosperous and fulfilling life, *Your Life by Design™*.

The achievement of one goal should be the starting point of another.
—ALEXANDER GRAHAM BELL

SECRET TO YOUR SUCCESS #4

—Dare To Be Bold: Expect Epiphanies

Fortune favours the bold.
—Virgil

AT 1 O'CLOCK IN THE MORNING ON AUGUST 9, 2014, I had an epiphany I want to share. But before I get to that, let me share the backstory.

The third edition of this book had just come out, and I had the same feeling I had always had about my book: I had done only a mediocre job of getting the book into the marketplace.

When I did give the book out, people immediately perceived me as more credible because my name was on the cover of a book. While business cards are quickly discarded, it's tough to throw away a book. Even if they are never opened, books tend to hang around as quiet reminders on desks, bookshelves, or nightstands. So within my immediate circle of influence, my book has been incredibly successful, helping me solidify relationships and build deep bonds with potential clients. In a crowded, commoditized business world, the book was helping me differentiate myself like never before.

Regardless, I felt like I should be doing a lot more to leverage the book for its content. I wanted more people to hear my message, even if they weren't within my immediate circle—even if they were never going to become clients.

I wanted to go big and bold.

During this same time, I was feeling inspired as I reread Rick Warren's incredible book, Purpose Driven Life. On August 8, I was reading the message from Day 38 of the book in which Rick challenges the reader to be more of a world-class Christian (focused on serving others) and less a worldly Christian (focused on ourselves).

I was struck by this contrast and asked myself where I was on the spectrum. It's so easy to get caught up in ourselves, our needs, our problems, our wants. I went to sleep that night with this on my mind.

At 1 a.m., I awoke with an idea that was bold and would help me be more of a world-class Christian.

The idea, which I brainstormed all the way until 5:30 a.m., and just about every day since, was to partner with some of the book's readers, many of whom have become incredible recommenders and great implementers of the book's strategies.

I thought that a few of these Life by Design champions might like to share some of their stories and the examples for how they implemented the book. Each new edition could feature one co-author, who shared his or her examples alongside mine. We could create multiple covers and various titles so that in every city, each book would be unique on the inside and the outside.

It occurred to me that in exchange for becoming a co-author of the book, which allowed them to experience the same benefits I had already experienced in terms of solidifying relationships and building deeper bonds, they might be willing to make an annual donation to one of our charitable interests.

In this way, every new co-author would help me get the message of the book into more hands and raise potentially significant donations for game-changing charities. In calculating the philanthropic opportunity, I started by focusing on my current coaching model, where clients make a $6,000 contribution to Whitworth University in exchange for one year of coaching with me. I figured that if I could find ten interested co-authors, we could raise an extra $60,000 each year for charity.

I would consider this a home run, but at about 2 a.m., I got an even bolder idea: I might be able to find fifty co-authors, which would allow us to give away $300,000 annually. Then, as dawn approached, I went exponential and dreamed of getting 170 co-authors on board, which could raise $1 million annually.

Wouldn't it be simply extraordinary to be part of giving away $1 million every year?

I am truly humbled to share that as of this printing, we already have the first ten co-authors signed up—and I have only just begun to share this plan in the last couple months. Another thirty are in various stages of the co-author application and interview process.

I have had interest from amazing individuals in all different industries who love the Life by Design message and who want to add their story and wisdom to a personalized edition of the book.

To support our co-authors in the publishing and book promotion process, Matt Burrow (matt.burrow@ biggerfuturespress.com) has joined our team as a partner and co-author mentor. Matt previously created and implemented the business development strategy for the largest law firm in the world. He exemplifies the vision for delighting our clients in every interaction.

ARE YOU LIVING YOUR LIFE BY DESIGN?
We love to partner with our readers who are living their life by design. To learn more about becoming a co-author of *Your Life By Design,* contact our co-author mentor Matt Burrow at **matt.burrow@biggerfuturespress.com.** Because we offer exclusivity based on geography, we hand-select the most qualified candidates to participate in our co-authorship program.

We have been asked to speak at multiple companies across the country, and I have two talks early next year to groups of 1,500 and 2,000.

What if we could have the first 100 co-authors by August 8, 2015? It's exciting to see what might happen as a result of putting pen to paper in the middle of the night when inspiration strikes.

Notes:

YOUR LIFE *by Design*™ COACHING OPTIONS

1. Do It Yourself

Use the official *Life by Design Manual*™
to complement the book.

> **Building Your Bigger Future**

↓

> **Creating Your Strategy**

↓

> **Implementing Your Strategic Plan**

↓

> **Transformational Results**

4. The Inevitable Success System

12 months of coaching with Curtis Estes to help you
complete the *Life by Design Manual*™ and provide
extra support and accountability in attaining
your most important goals.

2. Let Us Help

Two sessions with a certified coach to help
you complete the *Life by Design Manual*™

3. Just Show Up

Five personalized sessions with Curtis Estes to help
you complete the *Life by Design Manual*™

As a complement to this book, we offer assistance in designing your ideal life customized for your unique circumstances. To accelerate your progress, choose from one of four Coaching Options:

1. Do It Yourself—$19.95

Purchase the official **Life by Design Manual™,** which binds all the worksheets and templates you need to create an inspiring and ongoing tool for taking control and designing your life.

2. Let Us Help—$1,995

This includes the **Life by Design Manual™** plus two face-to-face sessions with a certified *Your Life by Design™* coach in which we speed up the entire process and help you finalize your **Life by Design Manual™**. Annual update sessions are available for $995.

3. Just Show Up—$4,995

This includes the **Life by Design Manual™** and five sessions with Curtis Estes in which he will direct you in each of the exercises and coach you in preparing the **Life by Design Manual™**. We deliver your completed plan in a leather-bound binder. Annual update sessions are available for $995.

4. The Inevitable Success System—$9,995

Research shows that systematic accountability generates five times more results, 50 percent sooner than working alone. For this reason, the Inevitable Success System includes all of the above with monthly coaching sessions over the course of a full year. You will set specific monthly action steps and get the extra support necessary to attain your most important goals. Annual updates available for $995.

Pricing as of January 2015 publishing.
For more information, visit
www.curtisestes.biz

RECOMMENDED READING & VIEWING LIST

There is no frigate like a book to take us lands away.
—EMILY DICKINSON

Recommended Reading

- *The Bible*

- *Jesus Calling* by Sarah Young

- *My Utmost for his Highest* by Oswald Chambers

- *The 21ˢᵗ Century Agent* and *The Advisor Century* by Dan Sullivan

- *Unique Ability*® by Catherine Nomura, Julia Waller, and Shannon Waller

- *Secrets of the Young and Successful* by Jennifer Kushell and Scott Kaufman

- *Get Out of Your Own Way* by Robert K. Cooper

- *Rhythm of Life and 7 Levels of Intimacy* by Matthew Kelly

- *Aspire!* by Kevin Hall

- *Miracle Morning* by Hal Elrod

- *Freedom Ratio* by David Fenton

- *The Other 8 Hours* by Robert Pagliarini

- *The Man in the Mirror* by Patrick Morley

- *Your Money Counts* by Howard Dayton

- *Money, Possessions, and Eternity* by Randy Alcorn

- *The Greatest Salesman in the World* by Og Mandino

- *Les Misérables* by Victor Hugo

- *Count of Monte Cristo* by Alexandre Dumas

- *Strong Fathers, Strong Daughters* by Margaret J. Meeker

- *Championship Fathering* by Carey Casey

- *The Power of a Praying® Wife* by Stormie Omaritian

- *The Power of a Praying® Husband* by Stormie Omaritian

- *Swim with the Sharks without Getting Eaten Alive* by Harvey Mackay

Recommended Viewing (Inspirational)

- *The Ultimate Gift*

- *Freedom Writers*

- *The Pursuit of Happyness*

- *It's a Wonderful Life*

- *Secret of My Succe$s*

- *Gladiator*

- *Meet Joe Black*

- *Schindler's List*

- *Life is Beautiful*

- *Dead Poet's Society*

Recommended Podcasts

- Andy Stanley: *yourmove.is*

- Mark Batterson: *theaterchurch.com/media/podcast*

- Mike Breaux: *vimeo.com/heartland*

- 10X talk with Joe Polish and Dan Sullivan: *10xtalk.com*

ABOUT THE AUTHOR

CURTIS ESTES, CFP®, BEGAN HIS CAREER IN 1991 with Northwestern Mutual, and in 1997 he became a founding principal of Strategic Benefits Group. He graduated from the University of Kansas with a degree in journalism. Curtis's focus is helping superstars create bigger futures. He does this by working with his clients to define their goals and dreams, then developing solutions to achieve these dreams.

Most American families spend hour after hour planning their vacations, but only 14 minutes a year addressing their financial needs, and Curtis is dedicated to helping them place at least as much intentionality on their financial picture as on their next holiday. As such, he considers life planning a critical complement of every family's financial future.

An avid proponent of philanthropy, Curtis is actively involved in the Bel Air Presbyterian Church, the Internal Justice Mission, and the National Center for Fathering. He is a trustee for Spokane's Whitworth University and a board member at Pacifica Christian High School.

Curtis lives in Los Angeles with his wife, Kristi; sons, Jordan and Christian; and daughter, Vyvien.